NAKSHATRAS
IN VEDIC ASTROLOGY

EASY & SIMPLE

Anatoly Malakov

ISBN 978-619-92565-1-0 (e-book)
ISBN 978-619-92565-0-3 (paperback)

Publisher- Anatoli Malakov

Contacts:
Email: astrology.coaching1@gmail.com

Website: www.astrology-coaching.com

YouTube channel and Facebook:
Astrology Coaching by Anatoly

Online Astrology Course for beginners:
https://astrologycoaching.thinkific.com

CONTENT

INTRODUCTION

Nakshatras are one of the most interesting and fascinating parts of Vedic Astrology. This is my favorite astrological field because it combines astrology, mythology, wisdom, and symbolism and describes individuals and their life in an incredible way.

Nakshatras, also known as Lunar mansions or constellations, are the basis of Jyotish (Hindu Astrology) and they tell more than you have ever imagined!

I have been studying nakshatras for years – I enrolled in many astrology courses, read multiple nakshatras books, analyzed nakshatras through the horoscopes of my clients and finally decided to create one simplified book, that explains easily and understandably the core of nakshatras.

This book "Nakshatras in Vedic Astrology- Easy & Simple" is a part of my **"Easy & Simple" series**, together with my other book – "Vedic Astrology- Easy&Simple"- and notebook "Vedic Astrology- Easy&Simple – The Notebook".

All these books are structured and written, especially for people who are beginners in Vedic Astrology. They are specifically made for all astrology lovers, who are new to this subject and need an "Easy & Simple" explanation of the complex essence of Vedic astrology. As I said before:

"I believe in the magic of simplicity… In order to dive deeply into the ocean of Hindu astrology, you need to know how to swim, right?"

So now it's your time to learn how to swim in the ocean of the mystical nakshatras....let's go!

CHAPTER 1
WHAT ARE THE NAKSHATRAS?

The first question that we need to answer is: "**What is the nakshatra?**". As I have written in "Vedic Astrology-Easy & Simple", the term "nakshatra" means "sky map" – the word "naks" means sky and the word "shetra" means region. So, nakshatras are the constellations (stars) that create the zodiac belt. The whole zodiac system is 360 degrees, and it is divided into 12 zodiac signs. These 12 zodiac signs are consisted of 27 nakshatras (27 constellations). Each nakshatra is 13 degrees and 20 minutes long and they start from 0 degrees Aries and end at 30 degrees of Pisces. Some nakshatras lie entirely in one zodiac sign, whereas others overlap in two zodiac signs, but always their length is 13°20'.

Additionally, each nakshatra is divided into 4 quarters, which we call Padas. Every Pada is 3 degrees and 20 minutes. Padas have their own energy and meaning, however, at this point, we will not focus on them, because we need to keep it Easy & Simple, but it is good to know this information for your future studies.

Nakshatras are also called Lunar mansions, because the Queen of the Planetary cabinet, Moon, resides in one nakshatra per day (approximately).

So now it is time to learn the "fairy tale" about the Moon and the nakshatras.... Maybe you are wondering why I am saying that? Mythology is the essence of nakshatras, and this is the reason I love them...nakshatras mix the mystical world of mythology with the practical knowledge of the material world.

So, the fairy tale goes like that.... The Moon in Vedic astrology is called Chandra, who is a gracious, handsome god. Chandra got married to the 27 daughters of sage Daksha, who was the son of Lord Brahma. These 27 daughters are the Nakshatras – Moon's wives. When Daksha married his 27 daughters, the Moon God promised him that he will treat his 27 daughters equally.

However, Chandra got fonder of his fourth wife, Rohini, and spent most of the time with her, which made the other 26 wives very angry (this is the reason why in Vedic Astrology we say that the Moon is exalted in Taurus, especially in the constellation Rohini....because Rohini is the favorite wife of Chandra).

So, the other 26 wives wanted equal love and care from Chandra, unfortunately, the Moon God ignored that, and the wives complained to their father. Daksha got angry and cursed the lunar deity to become ill and lose his brightness. Chandra begged Daksha to take the curse back, but it was too late.

After that Chandra went to Lord Shiva, searching for help. Lord Shiva explained to Moon-God that he can't reverse the curse of Daksha but can make it milder and from that day onwards, Moon increases its brightness for 14 days, which we call Waxing Moon, and decreases in brightness for 14 days - Waning Moon- and is obliged to spend one day with each of his wives!

So, this is the mythology story behind the Moon and the Lunar mansions and now maybe you are wondering what are the names of the beautiful wives of Chandra. The names of the Nakshatras are:

Ashwini, Bharani, Krittika, Rohini, Mrigashira, Ardra, Punarvasu, Pushya, Ashlesha, Magha, Purva Phalguni, Uttara Phalguni, Hasta, Chitra, Swati, Vishakha, Anuradha, Jyeshtha, Mula, Purva Ashadha, Uttara Ashadha, Shravana, Dhanishta, Shatabhisha, Purva Bhadrapada, Uttara Bhadrapada, Revati.

Please note that we will be using the **equal system of the nakshatras** – this is the most used system in Vedic Astrology. All of the notable Vedic astrologers use it.

There is another unequal nakshatra divisional system in Jyotish, which includes different degrees of some of the constellations and even 28 Nakshatras system. In this unequal nakshatra system, there are 15 nakshatras of normal length, the nakshatras Bharani, Ardra, Ashlesha, Swati, Jyeshtha and Shatabhisha are half of the normal length of 13°20' and the nakshatras Rohini, Punarvasu, Uttara Phalguni, Vishakha, Uttara Ashada and Uttara Bhadrapada are one and half times the normal length.

Of course, at the end of the book, I will provide you with more information about the unequal system, just to know it and not to get confused. This unequal system is not commonly used, however nowadays it got more popular, and I want people who are reading "Nakshatras -Easy &Simple" to be aware of this divisional system. The main aim of the book is to help beginners and make your study "Easy& Simple" because when I was studying astrology there were no books like that...books that present the information in a simple, practical, and useful way.

CHAPTER 2
NAKSHATRAS CLASSIFICATIONS

In order to understand nakshatras we need to know more about their essence. This is the reason, I will share with you the most important divisions and classifications of the Vedic constellations, which will help you to understand their logic, action, and power.

My recommendation is before going deeper into constellations- you need to get to know the basic of Vedic Astrology – planets, houses, zodiac signs and dashas. This will help you to understand the subject. You can read the books of Richard Fish and Rayan Kurczak, Kapiel Raaj, Joni Patry, and James Braha or you can check my book for beginners in Jyotish – **"Vedic Astrology -Easy&Simple"** on Amazon and my online video course for beginners in the platform of Thinkific: **Online Astrology Course for beginners**: https://astrologycoaching.thinkific.com

They will put a strong foundation for your Hindu knowledge, and you will be ready to go further into studying Jyotish.

Nakshatras classifications:

1. Division as per the ruling planet of nakshatras

- Sun ruled nakshatras – Kritika, Uttara Phalguni, Uttara Ashadha

- Moon ruled nakshatras – Rohini, Hasta, Shravana

- Mercury ruled nakshatras – Ashlesha, Jyeshta, Revati

- Venus ruled nakshatras – Bharani, Purva Phalguni, Purva Ashadha

- Mars ruled nakshatras – Mrigashira, Chitra, Dhanishta

- Jupiter ruled nakshatras – Punarvasu, Vishakha, Purva Bhadrapada

- Saturn ruled nakshatras – Pushya, Anuradha, Uttara Bhadrapada

- Rahu ruled nakshatras – Ardra, Swati, Shatabisha

- Ketu ruled nakshatras – Ashwini, Magha, Mula

The ruler of nakshatras is extremely important when you are analyzing horoscopes and the personality of an individual. For example, the nakshatra of the Ascendant will tell you a lot about the character of the person, together with the ruler of this nakshatra. Moreover, the position of the ruler of the Ascendant nakshatra in a person's natal chart will show you the destiny of this person. I will give you an example:

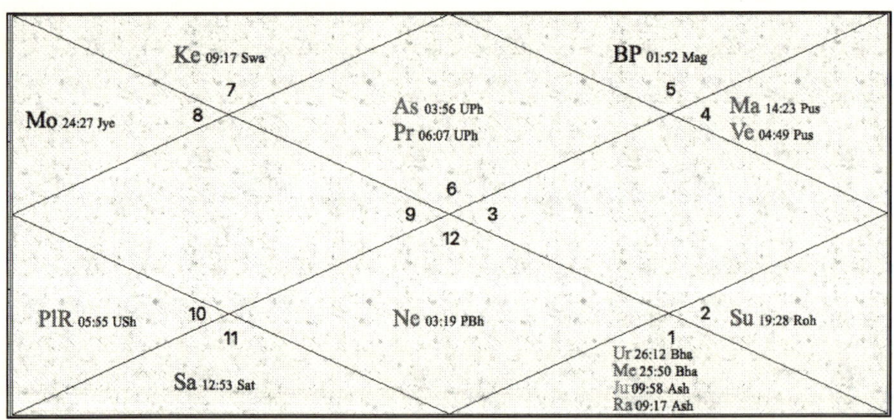

This is the natal chart of one of my clients- here you see that the Ascendant is around 3 degrees Virgo, which means that the Ascendant lies in the nakshatra

Uttara Phalguni. Uttara Phalguni is ruled by the Sun and the position of the Sun will give you more information about the life path and purpose of the person. The Sun is in the 9th house, so the dharma of the person is associated with the significations of this house and the zodiac sign Taurus, which occupies that house. The ninth house is religion, philosophy, optimism, education, father, guru, teachers and preachers, long-distance travelling, foreign cultures, laws, publishing, luck, and hope. Taurus is family and family values, resources, savings, nature, and finance. Of course, I am not going to analyze it now, I just wanted to show you how it works. Please note that this is only one of the many ways of finding a person's life path – you have to use the other techniques, too, in order to have a more detailed horoscope reading.

The ruler (Lord) of the nakshatras is used especially for determining your Dasha periods (Planetary periods). The hour that you are born will determine from which Dasha your life will start. You should check the position of the Moon and more specifically, the nakshatra of the Moon and its ruler. In the example above, we see that Moon is placed in Nakshatra Jyeshta- this means that the first planetary period of your life will be the one of Mercury because Mercury is the ruler of Jyeshta.

Some of the nakshatras are more auspicious and favorable than others, so the lessons that you need to learn will be different depending on the nakshatras you have in your chart. In my practice with astrology coaching and consultations, I have noticed that the nakshatras ruled by Rahu and Ketu are more difficult and bring a lot of ups and downs in life. Strangely, the same is the situation with the nakshatras ruled by Jupiter. Although Jupiter is the planet of luck and optimism, its nakshatras give a lot of karmic lessons. Maybe because Jupiter is Guru, a teacher and the teacher gives you lessons. On the other side, I have noticed that the nakshatras ruled by Saturn are easier and more prosperous, even though their ruler, Saturn, is the planet of delay, sorrow, diseases, hard work, and unprivileged people.

2. Division as per the Gana of the Nakshatras

Gana in Hindu astrology is something like a temperament of the nakshatra. Each nakshatra is classified as Deva, Manushya and Rakshasa.

Deva Nakshatras are God-like, and the belief system and the knowledge are the focus. Manushya Nakshatras are more Human-like and are driven to results and they are more pragmatic and practical. Rakshasa Nakshatra are Demon-like and are inclined to break taboos and destructions.

- Deva nakshatras are Ashwini, Mrigashirsha, Punarvasu, Pushya, Hasta, Swati, Anuradha, and Revati.

- Manushya nakshatras are Bharani, Rohini, Ardra, Shravana, Purva Phalguni, Purva Ashdha, Purva Bhadrapada and Uttara Phalguni, Uttara Ashadha, Uttara Bhadrapada

- Rakshasa nakshatras are Krittika, Ashlesha, Magha, Chitra, Vishakha, Jyestha, Mula, Dhanistha, and Shatabhisha.

3. Division as per the Trimurtis

Each nakshatra is associated with one of the Trimurtis - Brahma, Vishnu, Shiva, which are one of the most significant forms of Brahman, the Ultimate Reality. The word 'Trimurti' means 'three forms'- Brahma energy is to create, Vishnu energy is to maintain and preserve, and Shiva energy is to destroy and transform. Simply said, Brahma is the creator, Vishnu is the preserver and Shiva is the destroyer.

- Brahma- Ashwini, Rohini, Punarvasu, Magha, Hasta, Vishakha, Mula, Shravana, Purva Bhadrapada

- Vishnu- Bharani, Mrigashira, Pushya, Purva Phalguni, Chitra, Anuradha, Purva Ashadha, Dhanishtha, Uttara Bhadrapada

- Shiva- Krittika, Ardra, Ashesha, Uttara Phalguni, Swati, Jyeshta, Uttara Ashadha, Shatabisha, Revati.

4. Division as per the Motivation of Nakshatras

The motivation of the Nakshatras indicates the goal or the purpose of the Nakshatras:

- Dharma – to find the purpose of life.

- Artha – to find material well-being.

- Kama – to find fulfilment of your desires.

- Moksha – to find spiritual enlightenment and freedom from this material world.

Dharma nakshatras are Ashwini, Pushya, Ashlesha, Vishakha, Anuradha, Dhanishtha, and Shatabhisha.

Artha Nakshatras are Bharani, Punarvasu, Magha, Swati, Jyeshta, Shravana, and Purva Bhadrapada.

Kama nakshatras are Kirttika, Ardra, Purva Phalguni, Chitra, Mula, Uttara Bhadrapada

Moksha nakshatras are Rohini, Mrigashira, Uttara Phalguni, Hasta, Purva Ashadha, Uttara Ashadha, Revati

5. Division as per the Caste of Nakshatras

The caste, also known as Varnas, are:

- Brahmin- these are the priests, teachers, and other notable workers -they spread religion, and knowledge.

- Kshattriya- these are the worriers, and they protect and fight.

- Vaishya – a part of this caste is associated with the merchants, and they take responsibility to sustain and nurture through trade. The other part is associated with the farmers and workers in agriculture.

- Sudra- these are the servants, workers under authority and they are here to serve others.

- Ugra – these are the cruel workers like butchers.

- Chandal (Mleccha) – these are the outcaste, the unconventional

Brahmin are Krittika, Purva Phalguni, Purva Ashadha, Purva Bhadrapada.

Kshattriya are Pushya, Uttara Phalguni, Uttara Ashdha, Dhanishta, Uttara Bhadrapada.

Vaishya (merchant) are Ashwini, Punarvasu, Hasta

Vaishya (farmer/servant) are Mrigashira, Chitra, Jyeshta

Sudra are Rohini, Magha, Anuradha, Revati

Ugra are Adra, Swati, Mula, Shatabisha

Chandal are Bharani, Ashesha, Vishakha, Shravana

Please note that sometimes the different astrologers and astrological schools may give another division of the castes and the names of the caste. This depends on the different branches of Hindu astrology you follow.

6. Division as per the animal symbol

Animal Symbol	Male	Female
Horse	Ashwini	Shatabisha
Elephant	Bharani	Revati
Goat/Sheep	Pushya	Krittika
Serpent	Rohini	Mrigashira
Dog	Mula	Ardra
Cat	Ashlesha	Punarvasu
Rat	Magha	Purva Phalguni
Cow/Bull/	Uttara Phalguni	Uttara Bhadrapada
Buffalo	Swati	Hasta
Tiger	Vishakha	Chitra
Deer	Jyeshta	Anuradha
Monkey	Purva Ashadha	Shravana
Lion	Purva Bhadrapada	Dhanishta
Mongoose	Uttara Ashadha	-

CHAPTER 3
HOW TO USE NAKSHATRAS

As I mentioned at the beginning, nakshatras are one of the pillars of Vedic Astrology. The analysis of your personal nakshatras is very important. It will help you to figure out how you think, act, and understand life. You can use them for astrological predictions and analysis, checking the strength of your natal planets, analyzing current transits of planets through different zodiac signs and nakshatras, analyzing the eclipses of the Sun and Moon, learning more about your personal karma, physical and psychological traits, etc.

In Indian culture nakshatras and their deities are extremely significant. Indian people take into consideration the transit of the Moon through different nakshatras and what activities are favorable and unfavorable for that specific nakshatra. For example, there are a lot of people, who want to get married when the Moon transits through the nakshatra Uttara Phalguni because its deity is the God of patronage and friendship- Aryaman. It is said that Aryaman has a special connection to marriages. People, who have this nakshatra strongly presented in their horoscope charts, very often get involved in some kind of matchmaking, or weddings, they can become brides and brides men. For example, I have Uttara Phlaguni in my natal chart, and I was the one who met one of my girlfriends with her husband- it's a long story, but shortly said she was a little bit depressed, and I decided that I need to help her. I downloaded her a dating application, although she was against that, and I sent LIKEs to a few of the guys there. Afterwards, one of the guys, to whom I sent a LIKE, wrote to her and they started communicating. A few weeks later, on my day of birth (what a coincidence), they met

14

for the first time and fell in love. Now they are married for more than 5 years and have one beautiful child. I was a special guest at their wedding. Another example, I am the one who met my cousin with her husband. They are together for more than 10 years and they still tell me that I am their "Cupid". So, now you see how nakshatras in the horoscope explain your life to some extent.

One good idea- If you have the lord of the 10th house in Uttara Phalguni, you can try to create a dating application or matchmaking business, why not? Maybe it can work for you! Of course, I am a Virgo, and we need to be more practical- I need to say that you have to analyze everything in your chart in order to see the best career option, not only the nakshatras.

When you are analyzing nakshatras you have to take into consideration:

-   the different nakshatras classifications and their meanings,

-   the zodiac sign in which this nakshatra lies – for example, the nakshatra Mrigashira. It starts in Taurus, but ends in Gemini- it really matters, in which part of the nakshatra, your planet lies. In the Taurus, you will notice more Taurus and Venus energy, in Gemini- you will notice more Gemini and Mercury energy.

-   the ruling planet of the zodiac sign and the energy it has

-   the ruling planet of the nakshatra

-   the animal symbol of the nakshatra and its traits

-   most importantly, you have to consider the deity and the mythology, associated with that God. From my personal experience with astrological consultations, I realized that mythology is the core of the nakshatras. I am part of the Western civilization, and Hindu mythology sometimes is a little bit difficult for me, but I tried to extract in this book the most important key points from the nakshatras' mythological stories. Of course, we should keep it "Easy & Simple".

There are probably dozens of ways to use nakshatras. Different astrologers and astrology scholars have their own techniques and approaches. As a start, it is useful to analyze how the constellations influence your traits, behavior, and life. Then you can include them in your astrological predictions, Dasha analysis, transits, etc.

You should check the nakshatras of your birth Ascendant, Moon, Sun, Mercury, Mars, Venus, Saturn, Jupiter, Rahu, and Ketu. They will give you information about your life and characteristics. Of course, you can include the outer planets, too – Uranus, Neptune, Pluto- just please keep in mind that in Vedic Astrology, we use the outer planets for more worldly predictions or analyzing whole generations.

You should always keep in mind the significations of the planets!!! What I mean is that these planets and their nakshatras, not only give information about you, but they can also provide information about the things they signify in astrology and specifically in your natal chart. For example, Mars is an indicator of siblings, so through the nakshatra of Mars you can learn more about your siblings; Sun is an indicator of the father, Moon is an indicator of the mother, Venus is the karaka of love and so on. This is the reason, I mentioned at the beginning that you should have at least a basic knowledge of Jyotish in order to understand the essence of the Hindu constellations.

When I am doing horoscope readings, I always check:

- the nakshatra of the Ascendant

- the nakshatra of the Moon

The Ascendant and the Moon are significantly crucial for each horoscope. This is the reason you always have to analyze one chart from the Ascendant point of view and from the Moon point of view- Chandra Lagna (Moon Ascendant).

After that, it is important to check:

- the nakshatra of the Lord of the Ascendant – this is the ruler of the zodiac sign that occupies the 1st house and is extremely important for your life.

- nakshatra of the Dasha planet – this may tell you what kind of events, you can expect through the planetary period you are in.

Please note that nakshatras analysis is just a part of the whole analysis. You have to check the whole natal chart and the processes that are happening there – position of the planets, aspects, houses, zodiac signs, yogas etc., not only nakshatras.

If you want to know more about your love, you can check the nakshatra of Venus or the lord of your 7th house. Additionally – Jupiter is the significator of the husband in a woman's chart, so women can check the nakshatra of Jupiter in order to see the traits of their spouse, gay men can check the nakshatra of Mars to see their partner, men and lesbian women can check the nakshatra of Venus, which signifies love, but in men's and lesbians' charts signifies the wife, too.

If you want to know more about your life purpose and mission, check the nakshatra of your Rahu and Bhrigu Bindu point. If you want to know more about yourself, you can check the nakshatra of your Ketu, because Ketu is the karaka (indicator) of your past life and shows what you have brought to this life and you have expertise. So, Ketu will give you a lot of information about who you are, and what you have learned and will push you towards Rahu, your new mission.

You can check the Atmakaraka nakshatra (the planet with the highest degrees) – this is the soul indicator. The Karakas system is part of the Jaimini branch of Jyotish, and you can analyze your constellations through the meaning of the different karakas. Please note that this book is based on the most popular branch of Vedic Astrology - Prashara Hora Shastra.

If you want to know more about your career, you can check the nakshatra of the lord of the 10th house.

There are really dozens of approaches – I advise you to read more nakshatra books, test the different theories and methods in your personal life and see which one works for you.

CHAPTER 4
NAKSHATRAS

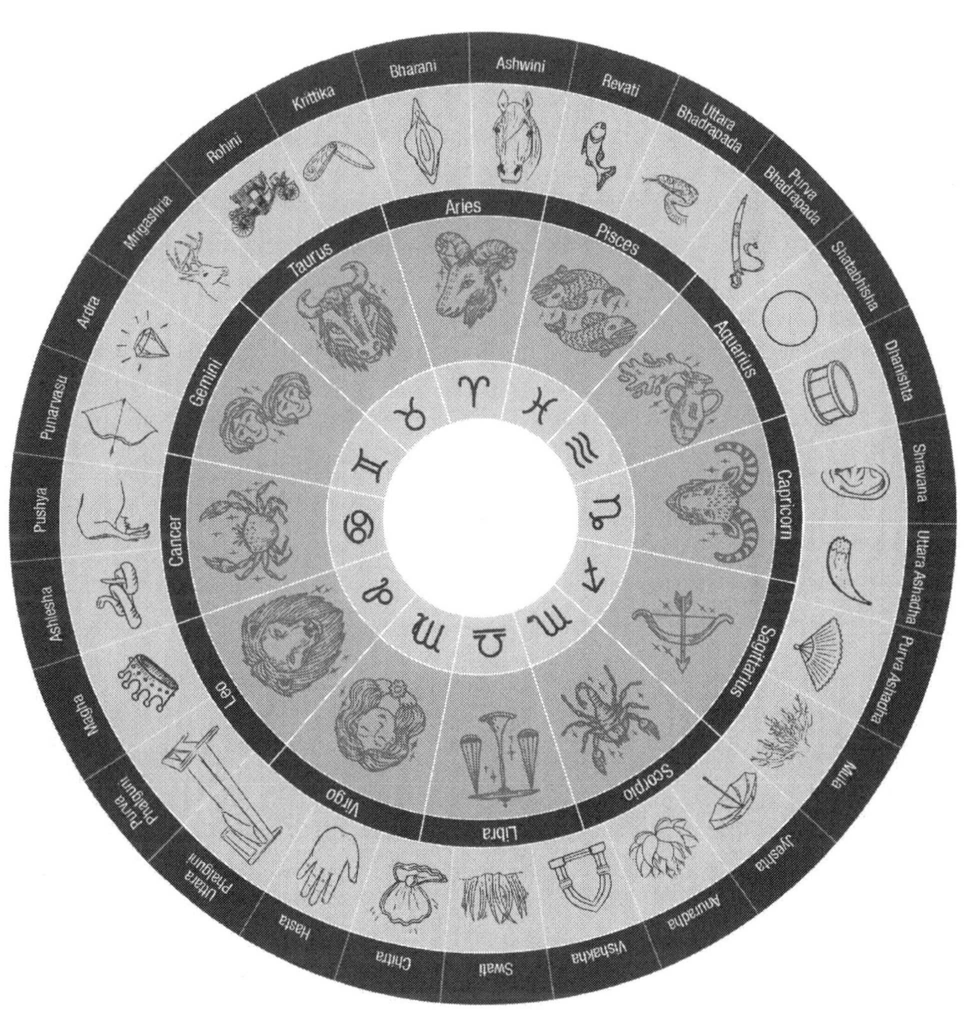

In the next pages, I am going to explain in an "Easy & Simple" way the core of all the 27 nakshatras and their most important characteristic. In order to understand the nakshatras you have to be familiar with the core meanings of the zodiac signs, and planets. It is good to learn more about the ruling deity, go deeper into the mythology associated with that God, analyze the symbol behind each nakshatra, the animal and what kind of character this animal has, and check the other classifications of the constellations.

I will include some additional information like Padas, sounds, color, gender, and fixed stars. They are important, too. For example, let's take the fixed star Spica, which is 29/30 degrees of Virgo, part of nakshatra Chitra. Spica gives sudden success, riches, and fame. If you have an Ascendant in Chitra nakshatra approximately 1 or 2 degrees around the fixed star Spica, this means 28-30 degrees Virgo, 0-1 degrees of Libra, you can expect sudden blessings, achievements, and popularity.

All of these factors are the background of the nakshatras. You cannot analyze a constellation without considering them.

Please note that each planet will have different qualities in the different nakshatras- Saturn in Ashwini is totally different from Sun in Ashwini. My advice is, as a beginning, to analyze your Ascendant and Moon nakshatras. Another important factor to consider - if there is a malefic influence over a nakshatra, its key traits may change to exact opposite!

ASHWINI

The Star of Speed

ZODIAC RANGE	0°0' ARIES - 13°20' ARIES
RULING PLANET	KETU
DEITY	ASHWINI KUMARS
SYMBOL	HORSE HEAD
CASTE	VAISHYA (MERCHANT)
ANIMAL	MALE HORSE
SOUNDS	CHU, CHEY, CHO, LA
MAIN FIXED STARS	ALPHA ARIETES/HAMAL BETA ARIETES/ SHERATAN GAMMA ARIETES/MESARTHIM
PADAS	PADA 1- ARIES, PADA 2- TAURUS, PADA 3- GEMINI, PADA 4- CANCER
COLOR	DARK RED/BLOOD RED
GENDER	MALE NAKSHATRA
KEY WORDS	HEALING, YOUTHFULNESS, TWINS, RAPID ACTIONS

Meaning

Ashwini is the first nakshatra in the zodiac belt. It lies entirely in the zodiac sign Aries. Ashwini brings the fiery energy of Aries and its ruler Mars, together with the spiritual and healing energy of Ketu, which is the ruler of that nakshatra.

What is Aries? Aries is impulsive, passionate, ambitious, and impatient, the baby of the zodiac belt. Aries is associated with ego, temper, speed, power, energy, and fights.

What is Mars? Mars signifies the same things as Aries- energy, aggression, impatience, impulsiveness, ambitions, and determination. Mars is the commander-in-chief in the planetary cabinet. Mars signifies medical fields, weapons, accidents, fights, etc. (Of course, I am mentioning just a part of the significations that are related in some way to the description of the nakshatra)

What is Ketu? Ketu is an indicator of spiritual enlightenment, detachment from the material world, healing, healers, occult, phobias, isolation, and psychic abilities. Ketu is a body without a head.

So now you can imagine what kind of energy this nakshatra contains as per the zodiac sign and associated planets.

Ashwini means "horsewoman" or "born from a female horse". The symbol of this nakshatra is a horse head and the animal is a male horse. The horse and everything that this animal symbolizes is a crucial part of Ashwini. The horse is a symbol of speed, movement, transportation, power, beauty, and elegance. It is connected to the seven horses of Surya (the Sun God). The seven horses also represent the seven chakras – and people with prominent planets in Ashwini nakshatra can experience the powerful kundalini energy.

I have noticed in my consultations that people who have Ascendants in Ashwini nakshatra have very beautiful hair- it's like a horse mane.

Deity

The Gods that are ruling this nakshatra are **Ashwini Kumars** (Dasra and Nasatya). They are twins, sons of Surya and they are called the divine doctors- healers of the Gods. Ashwini Kumars are illustrated as two humans with horse heads.

As I said, mythology is very important, when we want to understand the nakshatra. I will try to extract the most important mythological stories and explain them to you in an "Easy & Simple" way. Please note that when you read various Vedic nakshatras books, you will encounter minor differences in the mythological stories. In the beginning, when I was studying this subject, this confused me a lot, but apparently, each author has his style and translates the stories in his way.

<u>The Birth of Ashwini Kumars</u>:

Surya, the Sun God, was married to the daughter of Vishvakarma (Tvashtar)- Sanjana. She was in love with the Sun however, she could not bear the heat of the God. She decided to replace temporarily herself with a clone and created Chhaya, who took her place as Surya's wife. Then Sanjana went to her father. Sun didn't realize that this is not his wife and had children with Chhaya- Saturn, Manu, and Tapti. However, Chhaya showed more love towards her children rather than Sanjana's children- Manu, Yama, and Yamuna. Chhaya even cursed one of the children of Sanjana- Yama. Surya was surprised that a mother can curse her own child and confronted Chhaya who after this revealed the truth. Sun God loved Sanjana and started searching for her. Eventually, he found his wife roaming on the Earth as a horse. He transformed himself into a beautiful stallion and mated with her. And from the nostrils of the horse mother, the twins Ashwin Kumars were born.

Ashwini Kumars are divine physicians – great healers, who knew agriculture, herbs, and Ayurveda. They are also known to possess knowledge about horses. They are fond of honey (Madhu) and Soma. There are many mythological stories where the twins healed others. They cured the blindness of a friend, cured the blindness, rejuvenated, and restored the beauty and youthfulness of Chyavan Rishi.

Ashwini Kumars represent the twilight. They are invoked at dawn, before sunrise and it is believed that they descend to Earth to cure and restore the health of humankind. Ashwini Kumars used to have a flying chariot. This flying machine was either drawn by horses or by buffaloes. The flying machine exuded a golden glow and had a honey whip. It was full of honey and medicines and faster than light.

The Horse Head of Rishi Dadichi:

The King of the Gods, Indra, had one big secret – he knew how to produce a powerful elixir. He shared that secret only with Rishi Dadichi and cursed him that if he tells anyone how to produce this powerful elixir, his head will come off. Of course, Ashwini Kumars wanted to know the secret, so they made surgery and cut off the head of Rishi Dadichi and replaced it with a horse head. Then the horse head told the protected secret, and they turned back again the head of the Rishi. This again illustrates the unique medical abilities that these gods have.

Key Points

So, now I am going to explain to you how this nakshatra represents itself in our lives. This is for people, who have prominent Ashwini nakshatra in their astrological chart – especially if they have Ascendant and/or Moon in Ashwini. Of course, you have to check all planets and points, but, as I said each planet will mix its energy with the energy of the nakshatra and can modify its traits.

1. Ashwini natives are great initiators – they want to start something; they want to be the first to do something even though sometimes they don't analyze the situation and just go for it. This comes from the strong energy of Mars and Aries, which are warriors, fighters. If there is a battle, they will be the first ones to go! They will be the first to say YES to a new idea or adventure. So, if you are a manager and you need someone who wants to start a project in your company, you should find a person with prominent Ashwini nakshatra – this person will do it immediately!

2. Ashwini natives are free, passionate, impulsive, and sometimes, depending on the planet that is placed there, they can be very aggressive!

3. Ashwini natives are impatient – they cannot wait at all! They want everything now, at this moment. They don't like deadlines and orders. This is again the result of the energy of Aries.

4. Ashwini natives are great healers! All nakshatras ruled by Ketu have healing abilities. Furthermore, Ashwini is ruled by Ashwini Kumars – the healers of the Gods. People with prominent Ashwini nakshatra may have strong kundalini energy, know Ayurveda, and heal others with their powers or with herbs, or any plant-based medicine. Of course, they can

become great doctors. I recommend these people to grow their own herbs!

5. Ashwini natives are great opportunists – if they see an opportunity, they will grab it!

6. Ashwini people love speed, fast cars, and motors. They like drowns, helicopters, eagles, space, NASA, and rockets. Do you know why? You have to see the mythology – Ashwini Kumars had a flying chariot, faster than the light and human thought. They are fast – they eat fast, they talk fast, they walk fast.

7. Ashwini natives sometimes are like teenagers – youthful, funny, with a great sense of humour, and even sometimes they have this "prince-like" attitude. The reason for this is that Ashwini Kumars are the sons of the King – sons of the Sun, so they are princes! You will see that these people can have very easy-going youthful energy, they are spontaneous, like adventures and they can look young and fresh, no matter their age. Don't forget that Ashwini Kumars returned the beauty and the youthfulness of Chyavan Rishi – these people know how to rejuvenate themselves!

8. Ashwini natives can have twins, or they can be a twin. They can have a twin personality!

9. Ashwini natives like sports and movement.

10. Ashwini natives should pay attention to their noses, nostrils, and eyes. According to the mythology, Ashwini Kumars were born from the nostrils, and they poked the eye of a Rishi. This is the reason these people should be careful with these parts of their bodies, including their teeth. They can have a noticeable nose, too. On

the other hand, they can become ear, nose, and throat doctors.

11.   Ashwini people can be obsessed with their hair and appearance – they can be very fashionable. Don't forget that the horse is a symbol of that nakshatra, and horses are beautiful, with beautiful manes. They may have strong muscled legs and bodies, too.

12.   In the love field, Ashwini people are like a prince– they look for their princess and a big magical wedding. Generally, these people believe in love and desire it. After all, they were born out of the true love of the Sun and Sanjana.

13.   Ashwini people may have some family issues, especially if they have a planet that doesn't feel strong in this nakshatra. This comes from the story of Sun, Sanjana and Chayya. Siblings will play an important role in their life – favorable or not, depending on the whole natal horoscope of a person. They can even lose a sibling. Some Vedic scholars say that Ashwini natives can be born after miscarriages in their families.

14.   Sun is exalted in Ashwini and Saturn is debilitated. The reason for the debilitation is that Saturn is a son of the clone of Sanjana and was rejected by his father – the King Sun. Ashwini can create dictators! Hitler had an exalted Sun in Ashwini. It can bring disappointments, dissatisfaction, and mental and sexual issues if there are afflicted planets there.

15.   Ashwini people are not only good doctors, but they can become great merchants and bankers. The reason for that is their caste- Vaishya.

16. Ashwini people bring help and remove obstacles. They have fast intellect and an eye for the needs of other people. They have unique approaches; however, they tend to think that they deserve more from this life. Ashwini natives aspire for high positions, to be included among the elite, famous, and rich. This again comes from the mythological story of their deity. Ashwini Kumaras desired to drink the Soma (the Elixir of Life and Immortality) and to be considered equals amongst the Gods.

17. Ashwini people love the dawn, the sunrise. If you have strong planets in the nakshatra, you can have your spiritual practice early in the morning before sunrise.

18. Ashwini natives can be very knowledgeable in the field of agriculture, honey, and plants, so you can think of some business in these fields if you have prominent planets there. Honey and herbs can be very important for their health.

Remedies

As I have written in my book "Vedic Astrology-Easy&Simple", the Hindu remedies don't work on people, who don't have anything in common with the Hindu religion, culture, and philosophy. So, I am part of the Western world and will share remedies that are more practical and applicable to the people from Western civilization. If you want to improve your Ashwini nakshatra, you may take a statue or painting of 2 running horses, have a horse or go horse riding or you can do fasting when the Moon transits through Ashwini nakshatra. It is said that if you take medicine, while the

Moon is transiting Ashwini, the effect from the medicine will be faster.

Careers/Hobbies

Ashwini nakshatra may produce professions (or hobbies) related to:

- Horses or other animals– horse trainers, keepers, horse riding, horse breeding, animal keepers,

- Sports field – athletes and all sport-related jobs

- All kinds of healing and medical professions- physicians, therapists, herbologists, chemists, counsellors, physiotherapists, druggists, surgeons, Ayurveda or homoeopath specialists, veterinarians

- Cars, motors, airplanes, racing, transport industry

- Due to the strong Martian and Aries energy, you can see people in Law Enforcement Agencies, soldiers, policemen, engineers, physical arts, and physical professions.

- Professions that help other people, build the foundation, or start the beginning of something new.

- Professions related to agriculture and plants.

- Professions related to fashion and different fashion ornaments.

This is just a small list of jobs. You have to analyze much more things in your natal horoscope in order to understand the best career option for you. I will be honest, my nakshatras show more what are my interests, and hobbies, rather than what I had to do for a living. They give you a hint of what kind of career will give you happiness and joy, and why not money, but again....everything depends on the whole natal chart- not one nakshatra!

Example

I have decided to share some of the charts of my clients, just to give you an example, of how nakshatras manifest their power.

The following natal chart is a chart of a client (eventually a very good friend of mine) with Ascendant and Ketu in Ashwini. Apart from the fact that this person loves her car and loves driving fast, which is typical for the Ashwini natives, Ketu in its own nakshatra gives her incredible healing powers.

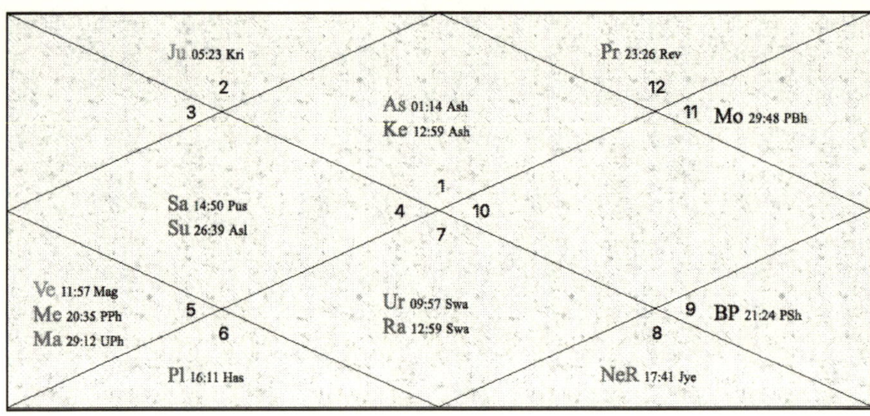

She has strong energy in her hands – they radiate warmth, which can heal. I remember she improved the eyesight of her child with this energy, she can heal headaches, calm the body, and relieve pain. Ketu gives her connection with other dimensions, in her case through dreams. Whatever she dreams becomes a reality. By the way, this is the reason why she came to me. She saw a video on my YouTube channel -Astrology Coaching by Anatoly- and in the evening she dreamt that I am calling her and that I would help her. She is a tarot reader, very good with herbs and oils, and has strong intuition.

I have another friend that has Sun and Mercury in Ashwini, and she is crazy about NASA, rockets, and Elon Musk. She is even thinking to relocate to Texas to watch all day the launch of the rockets.

BHARANI

The Star of Restraint

ZODIAC RANGE	13°20' ARIES - 26°40' ARIES
RULING PLANET	VENUS
DEITY	YAMA
SYMBOL	YONI (VAGINA)
CASTE	OUTCASTE
ANIMAL	MALE ELEPHANT
SOUNDS	LI, LU, LEY, LO
MAIN FIXED STARS	AL BUTAIN 35 ARIETES, 39 ARIETES, 41 ARIETES – THE DIM TRIANGLE
PADAS	PADA 1- LEO PADA 2- VIRGO PADA 3- LIBRA PADA 4- SCORPIO
COLOR	DARK RED
GENDER	FEMALE NAKSHATRA
KEY WORDS	CHANGE, TRANSFORMATION, DEATH AND REBIRTH, LABOR PAIN

Meaning

Bharani is the second nakshatra in the zodiac belt. It lies entirely in the zodiac sign of Aries. Bharani brings the fiery energy of Mars and Aries, together with the feminine energy and power of Venus, which is the ruler of the nakshatra.

We already learned what are Mars and Aries from the previous nakshatra Ashwini, so now we need to answer the question: "What is Venus? " Venus also known in Vedic Astrology as Shukra is the Guru of demons. It is the only planet that can bring back to life – it can resurrect from death. Venus is associated with females, love, romance, beauty, art, comfort, harmony, the reproductive system, the uterus, and semen.

So, Bharani nakshatra has one interesting Martian and Venusian energy, which makes this constellation unique.

Bharani means "bearer", "the one who bears," "labor pain", and also means "nurturing, supporting". The symbol of this nakshatra is a vagina. The three dim stars form a triangle in the sky, which looks like a female sexual organ. The vagina is a symbol of new life, death and rebirth, regeneration, resurrection, and transformation. The animal symbol is a male elephant. The elephant is related to many mythological stories and Gods like God Indra, lord Ganesha. It symbolizes power, size, strength, sexual drive, carrying a burden, transportation, and honor. The elephant is one of the most sacred animals in the Hindu world.

Deity

The God that rules Bharani is **Yama** – the god of Death. You have already heard about Yama in Ashwini nakshatra. Yama is a son of the Sun and Sanjana and was cursed by the clone of his mother- Chhaya. Maybe you are wondering why? The reason for the curse was that Yama felt unloved and ignored by his mother, without knowing that this is not his real mother, and kicked her in the belly with his leg. Chayya cursed him his leg to be filled with worms. After the truth about Chayya was revealed, the Sun helped Yama recover from the curse and blessed him to be the god of justice and righteousness.

According to the Vedas Yama is the first mortal, who died - he was killed in a war. His father, the Sun, then made him the God of Death. Yama guides humans to the world after death, the astral plane, and judges the departed souls -judge the good and bad deeds of the dead. Yama plays a vital role in preserving the balance of life and death. Yama is related to our ancestors.

Yama is associated with restrictions, self-control, principles and loyalty, and tolerance. Even his name means regulations, restrictions. Bharani is difficult nakshatra- it is associated with struggles, restrictions, and changes. It represents the difficulties that we need to face to succeed in life and grow.

Yama is illustrated riding a water buffalo, often with a mace in one hand, and an iron noose on the other.

Key Points

Now I am going to share with you some of the key traits of the natives, who have prominent Bharani nakshatra in their natal chart.

1. As I said, Bharani nakshatra is difficult and heavy nakshatra. People, who have many planets in this constellation or Moon and Ascendant, tend to face more difficulties in life. They have a sense of carrying a burden and

struggle to get what they want. Sometimes they may feel as if they are cursed, but if they are patient and self-controlled, they will be blessed! Remember Yama was blessed a few times by King Surya, and he became the God of justice and Death. So, these people should always remember that they need to go through the "labor pain" so they can be happy and evolve. After the pain, a new beginning comes, a new perspective. Extremely strong people, who can survive the storms.

2. Bharani natives face a lot of transformation, changes, death, and rebirth situations in their life. The old life needs to die for new life to begin. This constellation is associated with removing of the impurities and supporting everything alive.

3. Bharani natives have a special connection to the womb, sexual organs, and the whole reproductive system. If there are afflicted planets, miscarriages or health issues of the womb, vagina or other sexual organs can be seen. Bharani nakshatra produces many gynecologists.

4. Possible issues with their legs and belly– Yama was cursed, and his leg was filled with worms.

5. Bharani natives need a longer time to create something or finish something – this comes from the fact that pregnancy lasts 9 months and Bharani is associated with giving birth to something. Bharani will be the last to finish or arrive, their work is always delayed.

6. Bharani people have totally different points of view, and they differ from the surrounding world. This is due to their caste – Outcasts.

7. Bharani natives may have family issues – they may be adopted or feel like adopted, the mother can run away, the father can be more aggressive, problems with siblings. This is the result of the myth of the Sun, Sanjana and Chayya. We see the "twin" theme again because Yama had a sister twin -Yami. So, Bharani natives can have twins, or be a twin.

8. Bharani natives may have near-death experiences, and interests in cemeteries, graves, crows, life after death, occult. They can watch movies for reincarnations, astral travel, afterlife.

9. If there are no afflicted planets, Bharani natives will have strong bodies and prominent noses and teeth, due to the animal symbol of the nakshatra. They may have unusual eyes, too.

10. Bharani natives have a special connection with the dead people and their ancestors.

11. Bharani people, similar to their God Yama, follow the regulations, laws, and rules, and fight for the rights of other people. Justice is crucial.

12. Bharani natives can be extremely sexual, however depending on the whole natal chart, they can be restricted sexually at the beginning of their life and start their sexual life later than others. Addictions to sex, alcohol, food, and drugs may occur if there are afflicted planets here.

13. Bharani people have interests in Egyptian, Hindu, and Mayan cultures.

14. Bharani people can be very protective and nurturing of their children.

15.   Bharani people attract the attention of others, and they have powerful creative energy that comes from Venus.

16.   Bharani natives can be judgmental and arrogant in life, but they can become great lawyers and judges. They can be great initiators and pioneers, too.

17.   Bharani people can cause death and transformation to the world. This nakshatra can produce dictators if afflicted planets are placed.

18.   Bharani natives would often say phrases like "all done, I am finished, goodbye, I am done with you, I am finished with you."

19.   Bharani has a life-giving power!!! Don't forget this – not only giving a life to a child but giving a life to a project, books, songs, dreams, goals, etc.

Remedies

The best remedy for the Bharani people is to have a beautiful elephant statue in their home, but the trunks of the elephant should look up and should not be broken! If a person with a prominent nakshatra, ruled by an elephant, has issues with the teeth, this person will be unhappy! You should heal your teeth immediately! The power of the elephant is in the trunks, "its teeth"! Another remedy is to fast on the day when Moon transits Bharani. Of course, they are many other Hindu remedies with mantras and so on, however, I will share with you the more practical ones.

Careers/Hobbies

Bharani nakshatra may produce professions (or hobbies) related to:

- Childbirth, fertility, babies, and children- gynaecologists, obstetricians, babysitters, nannies, midwives, nursery teachers, workers in kindergartens, children's parks, amusement parks, toy industry, etc.

- Professions related to death, occultism, and funerals- morticians, coffin makers, occultists, etc.

- Professions involving sex, sexual energy, sex appeal and glamour- prostitutes, porn actors, dancers and striptease dancers, tantric experts, film and entertainment industry, workers in exotic night clubs, and models.

- Professions related to Laws and regulations – like lawyers, judges, and any professions related to courts.

- Professions that require secrecy – like detectives

- Professions related to the earth and the world under the earth- for example, the coal and petroleum industry, volcanic and earthquake experts, geophysicists, biologists, and microbiologists.

Example

I have had hundreds of clients and made hundreds of horoscopes, but I have never seen a chart like the one that I am going to show you now. This is a chart of one of my clients, who has a Moon in Bharani, and her life is a pure example of how Bharani manifests in the real world. I have even included that chart in the nakshatras lesson in my Online Video course for beginners in Vedic astrology:

link: *https://astrologycoaching.thinkific.com*

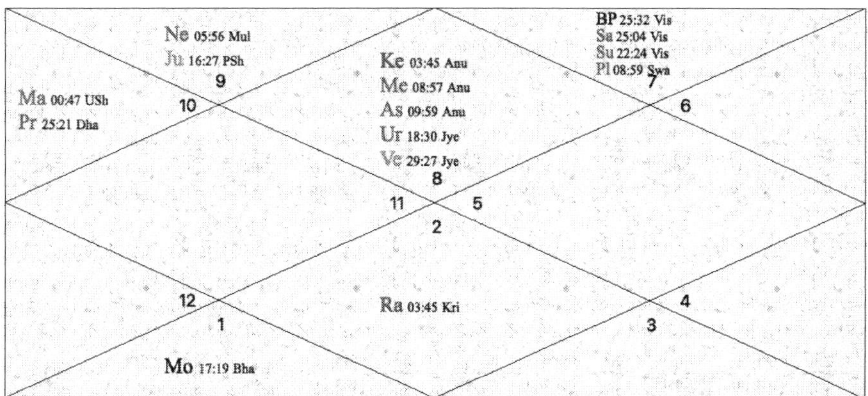

So, as you probably remember Bharani is associated with the womb, giving birth, death, and rebirth. My client experienced all of that. Let's start with the first Bharani manifestation. A few years ago, my client got pregnant. However, the pregnancy was a bit strange and one day she started bleeding a lot and went to the hospital. The nurses told her she most likely had a miscarriage and the fetus was lost and they had to clean out her uterus. She accepted the loss and went on with her life. One month passed, and the second month passed, but instead of getting slimmer, she got bigger and she thought she was sick. She went to another doctor to see her health status and the doctor was shocked, he even thought she was joking with him- it appeared that she is still pregnant. It turns out that her uterus is bicameral (bicornuate uterus) and she did not lose the baby- the bleeding was a normal biological process for such type of uterus and the doctors cleaned the empty chamber, not the one with the baby. It was like a miracle. Now her child is over 5 years old, alive and healthy. I hope I told the story understandably; I am not a specialist in biology; however, this is a typical Bharani story that involved the womb, baby, death, and rebirth.

The other unique story of the same client is related to her cat. Once her cat got very sick and the veterinarian told her, that the animal has some virus and will die and cannot be saved. Then she took the difficult decision to euthanize the cat in order not to suffer. She cried a lot in the clinic and the veterinarian saw the pain and felt very emotional. When she left, he decided to try to save the cat, without telling my client. After one week the cat was saved – alive and healthy. The doctor called my client to come and take her cat. This is another Bharani miracle – death and rebirth.

I hope you liked the stories – in my whole practice, I have never seen such powerful Bharani manifestations. Furthermore, my client is a lawyer – another Bharani trait!

KRITTIKA

The Star of Fire

ZODIAC RANGE	26°40' ARIES - 10°00' TAURUS
RULING PLANET	SUN
DEITY	AGNI
SYMBOL	RAZOR (A KNIFE)
CASTE	BRAHMIN
ANIMAL	FEMALE SHEEP (GOAT)
SOUNDS	AA, EE, OO, AE
MAIN FIXED STARS	THE PLEIADES (ATLAS, ALCYONE, MEROPE, ELECTRA, PLEIONE, TAYGETA, MAIA).
PADAS	PADA 1- SAGITTARIUS PADA 2- CAPRICORN PADA 3- AQUARIUS PADA 4- PISCES
COLOR	WHITE
GENDER	FEMALE NAKSHATRA
KEY WORDS	SHARP, CUTTING, PROTECTING, HEROIC, DETERMINED

Meaning

Krittika is the third nakshatra in the zodiac belt. It overlaps two zodiac signs – Krittika starts at 26°40' Aries and ends at 10°00' Taurus. This constellation has an interesting mixture of energy- from the Aries part, you feel the fiery energy of Mars and Aries, combined with the powerful energy of the Sun, which is the ruler of this nakshatra. On the Taurus part, the fiery energy transforms into a mix of earthy, practical energy and Venusian artistic energy, all influenced by the Sun.

We already know what Aries, Mars, and Venus are from the previous two nakshatras, so it's time to learn what are Taurus and Sun. Taurus is stable, solid, and associated with wealth, money, resources, values, family, family values, art, culture, poetry, nature, food, security, and searching for security. What is Sun? Sun, also known as Surya, is the King in the planetary cabinet- it is the soul, identity, personality, health, fame, success, father, authority, self-respect, dignity, and heart.

When you are analyzing a horoscope with prominent Krittika nakshatra, you should always pay attention, which part of Krittika is activated- the Aries or the Taurus one. There is a difference in the energy. Sun feels happy in Aries, together with Mars they create a huge passionate flame! On the other hand, the Sun, the ruler of the nakshatra, has animosity with Venus, the ruler of Taurus[1] and this creates more complex energy.

Krittika means "The one who cuts" or "The Cutters."

The symbol is a razor or a sharp instrument like a knife, which symbolizes the process of cutting, penetration, and the process of dividing. The razor has both constructive and destructive power- it can help you

---

[1] Venus and Sun are in different planetary camps – please refer to "Vedic Astrology- Easy&Simple", chapter 4.

build something or save your life, still, it can kill someone, too. The animal is a female sheep (goat), which is related to different mythological stories about Agni, who is illustrated riding a sheep, and Lord Shiva.

When you have a horoscope consultation, Krittika is one of the nakshatras, in which fixed stars play a significant role. That's why I am going to explain a little bit more about them. I mean, all fixed stars are important- don't get me wrong, but these are more specific. The Pleiades, which are located approximately 5°/6° of Taurus are called "The Seven sisters" or "The weeping sisters", which indicates sorrow and crying. If you have a client with planets around these degrees (plus-minus 1°or 2°), this person can face sorrow and pain in his life. At around 6° Taurus is Alcyone, which is one of the Pleiades. Some astrologers call this fixed star the Star of Sorrow, others- the Star of Prominence. But what is interesting is that this star has strong Venusian feminine energy- it is connected to beauty, creative arts, and femininity. Alcyone is associated with metrosexuality and homosexuality. If this star is prominent in a natal horoscope, it can produce feminine, metrosexual or homosexual people. David Beckham has Ascendant at 4° of Taurus and is strongly influenced by this star. He is a symbol of metrosexuality.

Another important fixed star, associated with Krittika is Algol – approximately 2 ° Taurus. This is one of the most evil stars – it deals with decapitation or losing your head. Algol is the head of Gorgon Medusa. So, if you have planets in Krittika (the Taurus part of the nakshatra), you should definitely check their degrees and be careful.

Deity

The ruling deity of Krittika is **Agni-** the God of Fire. Agni is the God of the sacred fire, the purifying fire that cleans and purifies the souls. He is the flame of aspiration and intellect, that illuminates and makes the world bright. Agni causes the fire of life. It is also the spark of life. Without fire, creation would not exist.

Agni and his child:

In order to understand the Krittika constellation, you need to know the story of Agni and his child Krittikeya. Please note that this story differs in the various Hindu sources. So, Agni fell in love with the wives of seven sages and transformed himself into a household fire to watch their beauty. A Goddess, named Shava, was in love with Agni and decided to take the appearance of the wives of the sages and make love with Agni. She transformed herself six times into 6 of the sages' wives and each time Shava planted Agni's semen into a lake in the mountain. She could not take the appearance of the 7th wife - Arundhati, who was so devoted to her husband, that even Goddess Shava didn't have enough power.

Meanwhile, the demon Tanaka conquered all Gods and start ruling the world. He had a curse that only a seven-day-old child can defeat him. Gods tried to have children so they can take back the authority, but they couldn't. Then the Goddess Ganges learnt that Agni's semen is planted in a lake in the mountain, and she added Shiva's seeds. Then a ferocious, powerful child was born and started destroying everything. The inhabitants blamed for that the 6 wives of the sages, called Krittikas, without knowing the real truth about Shava. Sages divorced their wives and sent them to tame the child and kill him. However, they felt compassionate about the child and accepted him as their own – called him Krittikeya. He split himself into 6 forms, so he can be nursed by the 6 wives. Then Krittikeya was tamed and greeted his father, Agni. When the child was 7 days old, the Gods put him in charge of their army, and he killed Tanaka.

Another important story is that Krittikeya told his 6 mothers that until he is 16 years old, he will be an evil spirit, that kills and eat children. Due to this mythological story, Krittika nakshatra is considered inauspicious for children and childbirth.

<u>Agni and the demon:</u>

A demon, called Rakshasa, desired the wife of a sage Brigu. This demon came upon Agni and demanded to know where the sage and his wife live. Agni was well known for not being able to tell lies and for his power to go into the hearth fire of every home. Agni told the Rakshasa where this woman lived. The sage cursed Agni and said he would be an 'omnivore', and would consume everything, pure and impure. Agni protested this curse and disappeared from every hearth. The world went dark and cold. Brahma found Agni and told him that he will soften the curse and no matter what Agni burns, the God of fire would remain pure and everything he burns, both pure and impure, would be purified. Then Agni returned.

Key Points

1. Krittika natives are strongly influenced by the Sun and its significations -they want to be the King; they are very individualistic and have an ego. These people want to rise in life.

2. Agni gives them hunger for something – this can be a hunger for food or hunger for success, love, or pleasures. The reason for that Krittika trait is one Hindu myth where Agni was cursed with an insatiable appetite.

3. Krittika natives can be very critical, very straightforward, and short-tempered. They can "cut" with words, they don't like lying and try to tell the truth, which can sometimes insult other people. They can be like a spoiled child. This comes from the mythology stories.

4. Krittika natives are very passionate – they have fire in their blood and heart. They have anger, which can destroy the world around them. Remember Krittikeya?

5. Krittika people have a passion for knives, swords, razors, or weapons.

6. They love cooking and cutting things. You can see many chefs with prominent Krittika nakshatra.

7. Krittika natives love adventures, love traveling the world and often go South- this is due to mythology stories, related to Agni.

8. Krittika people are fighters and spiritual warriors! They fight for social causes and want to destroy "Tanaka"- the demon, the evil. If they have a mission, they will give everything to fulfil it. However, at least once in their life, they will fail in a challenge they have accepted.

9. Krittika natives may face life situations connected to divorce, abortion, adoption, surrogacy, single or communal parenting, unusual pregnancy, childbirth issues, foster children and animals. These people may feel adopted or can have a stepmother/stepfather or they can become step-parents.

10. Krittika people love fire, barbeques, smoke, and tobacco. They may love to bite in sex.

11.   Number 6 plays an important role in their life. Remember Agni's child story - the six wives and the six forms of his child.

12.   Number 16 is another important number for this nakshatra. Somehow this number will play a role in the Krittika native's life- for example, when they are 16 years old some event can happen that may change their lives.

13.   Krittika natives are full of energy and charisma, they have the fire to purify and create! Extremely creative people, especially on the Taurus side.

14.   Krittika natives are associated with seduction and will try to seduce someone married or they can be seduced. They can have issues related to secret affairs and relationships.

15.   Krittika natives can be sperm or ovum donors. If there are afflicted planets, the natives may have issues with their semen/ovum.

16.   Krittika people love forests, trees and climbing mountains. They love food and eating. Some of them may love sheep or goat meat and milk.

Remedies

The best remedy for Krittika nakshatra natives is to have some kind of fire ritual or light candles in their homes. If they feel sad, they can go outside among nature and light a fire or have a barbeque, be among trees and forests.

Another remedy is to have a beautiful knife or sword in their home. I know from my astrology teachers, that when Krittika natives have fights in their home or work, they should cut one fruit in the middle with a sharp knife – this will soften the problem and even can fix it.

Careers/Hobbies

Krittika nakshatra may produce professions (or hobbies) related to:

- Fire – professions like a fireman or working in a Fire Department. Creative Arts involving the use of fire – jewellers, glassmakers, and fire dancers.

- Food and cooking

- Professions related to sharp instruments, knives, and razors – like swordsmen and blacksmiths. All types of technical professions. This may include barbers, hairdressers, and tailors, which use sharp instruments and cutting- in this case, barbers cut your hair and beard.

- Managers and people in authority positions

- Profession related to sharing opinions, and feedback -something like critics, commentators.

- Professions related to adoption, surrogacy, and donation of semen/ovum.

- Professions related to purifying and spirituality – like spiritual teachers.

- Military - generals and commanders, soldiers

Example

Famous people who have Krittika nakshatra are Frida Kahlo, Bob Dilan, David Beckham, and Bill Clinton. For example, Frida Kahlo has her Moon at 7° Taurus, which is influenced by the fixed stars –"The weeping sisters" – which causes pain and sorrow in her life. We see the number 6- she was born on the 6th of July, and she contracted polio at the age of 6 and this influenced her life; Another important thing is her unique Venusian and feminine creative energy and art. She became famous, not only for her talent but for her outspokenness and bravery; she was a fighter. Kahlo had a few miscarriages, never had children and her husband had multiple secret affairs. All of these are manifestations of Krittika.

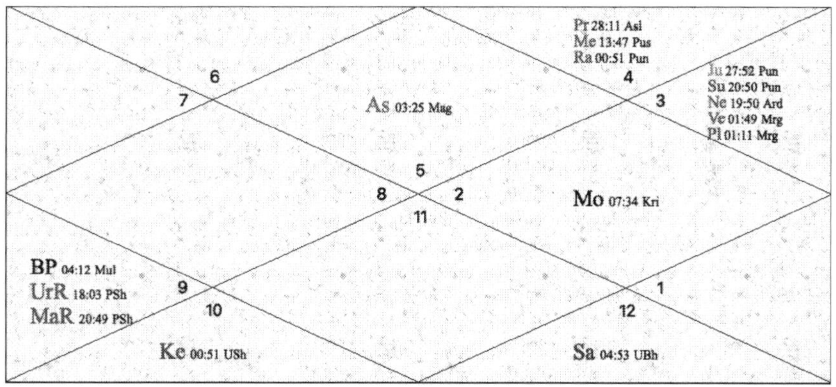

ROHINI

The Star of Ascent

ZODIAC RANGE	10°00' TAURUS - 23°20' TAURUS
RULING PLANET	MOON
DEITY	BRAHMA
SYMBOL	CHARIOT /OX-CART
CASTE	SHUDRA
ANIMAL	MALE SERPENT (COBRA)
SOUNDS	OH, VA, VE, VU
MAIN FIXED STARS	ALDEBARAN
PADAS	PADA 1- ARIES PADA 2- TAURUS PADA 3- GEMINI PADA 4- CANCER
COLOR	WHITE
GENDER	FEMALE NAKSHATRA
KEY WORDS	BEAUTY, WEALTHY, ARTISTIC, CREATIVE

Meaning

Rohini is the fourth nakshatra in the zodiac belt. It lies entirely in the zodiac sign Taurus. The planet that rules this constellation is the Moon, the Queen in the planetary cabinet. What is the Moon? Moon is associated with mother, females, fertility, emotions, feelings, mind, sensitivity, fame, reputation, masses, recognition, happiness, and general well-being. In Vedic Astrology, Moon is the most important planet. In Hindu culture, Moon is related to God Chandra – the Moon God, who loves beauty, luxury, and love. So, Moon is not only the mother, but it can be lustful, too – depending on the zodiac sign, position in the chart and nakshatra. Moon is exalted in Rohini and feels very powerful. Probably you remember the myth that I told you at the beginning of the book about Chandra and his 27 wives, called Nakshatras. Rohini was Chandra's favorite wife- she was famous for her beauty, artistic talent, and erotic art.

So, this constellation has one special, beautiful, and artistic energy, influenced by Taurus, Venus, and Moon. Rohini is said to be one of the most favorable nakshatras regarding earthy life.

Rohini means "The Reddish one" or "The Growing one". The symbol is a chariot or ox-cart, some astrologers even say that the symbol is a bull, pulling a cart. The chariot signifies power, respect, honor, and all kind of conveyances – it was the transport of all Gods. The ox-cart is a symbol of fertility, fruitfulness, and material success. The bull symbolizes strength, stability, productivity, and power. The animal that rules Rohini is a male serpent, which symbolizes spiritual power and wisdom. Of course, snakes can be vicious, dangerous, mesmerizing, and hypnotizing others to achieve their desires.

The fixed star Aldebaran, which is around 14° Taurus, is one of the brightest stars in the sky. It gives honor, popularity, and wealth, however, if you have planets around this degree, you should be careful, because this star can bring violence and sickness, too. You should not become too materialistic and there has to be a balance between the spiritual and material world.

Deity

The God of Rohini is **Brahma**- the God of Creation. He is the creator of the Universe and one of the main Hindu deities. This is the reason why Rohini is a nakshatra of creation and has powerful creative energy.

There are different Hindu myths related to Rohini – one of them you already know – Chandra and his 27 wives, the other is associated with Brahma. The legend says that Brahma, the creator of everything, created a daughter, called Rohini, but he fell in love with her. He started chasing her; however, he was stopped by Shiva, and he remained just a ruler of this nakshatra. From these myths, it is clear that Rohini has extraordinary charm and magnetism, and she is the most attractive one, so even Gods chase after her.

It is interesting to mention, that according to Hinduism, Brahma was born before anyone else and (almost) everyone was born from him. That's why the often-used name for Brahma is Prajapati – the original father. All of Brahma's creations came directly through his thoughts. This is the reason why Rohini natives are full of ideas.

Brahma is usually depicted on a lotus flower with four faces, the symbol of the four Vedas (collections of poems and hymns), the four yugas (ages), and the four directions. He is usually shown with four arms, too. Brahma was the first God in the sacred Hindu trinity or Trimurtis. The other gods are Vishnu and Shiva.

Key Points

1. Rohini natives are extremely creative – they are very artistic and full of ideas and talents. After all, they are children of Brahma – the creator. They are very productive, and love music, dancing, theatre, and all kind of arts.

2. Rohini natives are beautiful, sensual, and attractive – especially if they have Ascendant in Rohini. They are sexy, charming, and seducing, people are chasing them and want them. They love sex and screaming (not only in sex). They enjoy giving sexual pleasure to their partners. The sex with Rohini natives is always very hot and their partners remember them. However, if there are malefic planets here, Rohini natives can become narcissists, sex addicted, male and female prostitutes, porn actors, seducing and hypnotizing people for money and power – all negative traits of the snake will take over the good qualities of the nakshatra.

3. Rohini natives like the red color. If the native wants to seduce someone, he/she should put on red lipstick or red nail polish or a dress (red t-shirt for men or something red). This color will empower the nakshatra.

4. Rohini natives have specific eyes – they love makeup.

5. Rohini natives are meant to feel the life on the Earth, they are here to live on this planet – they are very earthy nakshatra and attached to this world. They should enjoy life on Earth and be present, be grounded like Taurus. Rohini is one of the most enjoyment-oriented nakshatras.

6. Rohini natives may have a love (or fear... depending on the planet) for snakes or reptiles.

7. Due to the different myths, Rohini natives may have a child that will be unmarried. This comes from the fact that the only child of Chandra is a result of cheating.

8. They love expensive cars and love traveling. As you know, the symbol of the nakshatra is a chariot.

9. Rohini natives can be bisexual – all snake-ruled nakshatras may produce bisexual people.

10. Rohini natives should be careful with people with prominent Uttara Ashadha nakshatra, which symbol is a mongoose! Mongooses eat cobras!

11. Rohini people love spying on other people, especially their partners. Issues with jealousy and possessiveness.

12. Rohini natives may be rich, wealthy, and popular. However, indulgence in materialism and luxury can lead to diseases and failures.

13. Rohini people wax and wane like the Moon- they are sometimes moody, restless, and wandering.

14. Rohini natives may have inappropriate relationships, which can get them into trouble in society.

15. Rohini natives may love gardens and nature and may have business in agriculture, business with cattle. This comes from the symbol of the nakshatra – ox-cart, which is related to the transportation of the earth's crops and fruits.

16. Rohini natives can be very "fertile" in all senses of the word. They can materialize their ideas and make them grow (Rohini means "The Growing One"). They can be very successful.

Remedies

The best remedy for Rohini people apart from fasting when Moon is transiting the constellation, is to have s photo or statue of a cobra. The other thing is to always clean their car and have a beautiful expensive car.

Careers/Hobbies

Rohini nakshatra may produce professions (or hobbies) related to:

- Arts - musicians, singers, poets, painters, actors,
- Professions related to the entertainment and leisure industry, fashion, beauty, and cosmetic industry.
- Sex – sex workers, erotic dancers, sex therapists
- Agriculture, liquids, food, plants, and animals
- Transportation, tourism, and cars

Example

Famous people who have prominent Rohini nakshatra are Marilyn Monroe and John F Kennedy. Merilyn Monroe is the first sex symbol in the movie world. She was attractive, sexy, and seducing... even "the God", The president of the USA, chased her ... typical Rohini.

MRIGASHIRA

The Searching Star

ZODIAC RANGE	23°20' TAURUS - 6°40' GEMINI
RULING PLANET	MARS
DEITY	SOMA, THE MOON GOD
SYMBOL	HEAD OF A DEER
CASTE	FARMER
ANIMAL	FEMALE SERPENT (COBRA)
SOUNDS	VAY, VO, KAA, KEE
MAIN FIXED STARS	EL NATH, LAMBA ORIONIS, BELLATRIX
PADAS	PADA 1- LEO PADA 2- VIRGO PADA 3- LIBRA PADA 4- SCORPIO
COLOR	SILVER GREY
GENDER	FEMALE NAKSHATRA
KEY WORDS	SENSITIVITY, SEARCHING, TRAVELLING, BEAUTIFUL

Meaning

Mrigashira is the fifth nakshatra in the zodiac belt. It overlaps two zodiac signs – starts at 23°20' Taurus and ends at 6°40' Gemini. This constellation, on one side, has the energy of Taurus, Venus, and Mars, which is the ruler of this nakshatra. On the other side, has the restless, quick energy of Gemini, its ruler Mercury, and Mars, Mrigashira's ruler planet. Mrigashira is a unique combination between the earthy, feminine energy of Taurus and the chameleon, inquisitive energy of Gemini. The Taurus side enjoys more the comforts of life, while the Gemini side is more restless and thinking- a more active mind.

What is Gemini? Gemini is associated with all kinds of communication, short traveling, art, and hand skills, it is restless, quick, flexible, adaptable, youthful, sexual, and likes humor and flirting.

What is Mercury? Mercury is the prince in the planetary cabinet. It is associated with communication, intelligence, speech, education, publishing, skills, business, healing, logical mind, humor, and friends.

Mrigashira means "A head of a deer" or "Benevolent". The symbol of this nakshatra is a deer's head. So, this animal is of great importance for that lunar mansion. The deer is a symbol of beauty, love, romance, wandering, fragility, and timidity. Deer are enchanting creatures, that always search for food and safety. This is the reason that the keyword for Mrigashira is "searching". The word "mriga" represent forest, a forest animal, seeking to find. The animal symbol of this nakshatra is the female serpent (cobra). Snakes represent secret knowledge and the concept of regeneration. They can be poisonous, too.

Some astrologers believe that this nakshatra has a neutral gender – it can be both male and female. Again, the reason for that is mythology – on one hand,

Mrigashira is ruled by the male god Soma, on the other hand, Mrigashira is associated with Parvati, the wife of Shiva. It is said that Parvati has her Moon in Mrigashira nakshatra. That's why the nakshatra has dual-gender energy.

Mars is the ruling planet- it gives courage, ambition, energy, and intellect. Mars can make this nakshatra very active. Combining Martian energy with Mercurian energy, people born in Mrigashira can become great thinkers and strategists, dangerous communicators.

Deity

The main God of Mrigashira is the Moon God - **Soma**. Soma is synonymous with Chandra. He is not only a manifestation of the Lunar God, but Soma is associated with the elixir of immortality, that Gods drink. This elixir, also called Amrita, grants eternal youth and power. Soma is associated with a plant, named as per some sources "Soma-Valli", which produces the elixir, that God drinks.

According to mythology, Soma's brother is the fire god Agni and Soma's sister is Rohini. The two brothers stand on both sides of their sister. It is said that the fire of Krittika, which is ruled by Agni, and the soma of Mrigashira, which is ruled by Moon God, makes Rohini nakshatra so fertile – Rohini stands between her brothers.

Another important myth is related to the love affair of Soma and Tara, the wife of Brihaspati (Jupiter). Legend says that Soma and Tara fell in love and had an affair. This caused a great war in Heavens between Brihaspati and Soma. Brahma intervened and stopped the war. Tara returned to her husband, but she was already pregnant. She gave birth to a child, called Buddha, also known by you as Mercury. This is the reason why in astrology planet Mercury accepts planet Moon as his enemy. Mercury is an illicit child and a result of the infidelity of Tara with Soma. So, when you are doing a horoscope reading, you should know that Mercury will almost always create some issues if it is associated with the Moon (through aspects, conjunctions, etc.).

Moon God is famous for his romantic stories, love encounters, and cheating, too. There is another story associated with this nakshatra – the story of the Golden deer. There was a demon, who fell in love with the wife of Lord Rama- Sita. He transformed himself into golden deer. Sita was so mesmerized by the deer that she couldn't resist it and the demon took her away. Eventually, Rama defeated the demon and took his wife.

As you can see, Mrigashira is associated with a lot of themes related to marriage problems, cheating, chasing others and being chased. Another theme is suicide. In a few words, just to keep it Easy and Simple at this point, as per the mythology, the daughter of Daksha, Sati married Shiva, however, Daksha didn't like Shiva. Daksha invited all Gods, except his daughter and her husband, to a special ritual in front of a sacred fire. His daughter came uninvited, and Daksha humiliated her in front of all Gods. Then she jumped into the fire and commit suicide.

Key Points

1. Mrigashira natives are always searching for the "elixir of life"– seeking security, love, and happiness. The whole process of searching is important. The searching can transform into chasing or stalking – chasing other people, goals, dreams, etc.

2. Mrigashira natives may love drinking or taking other substances. If there are malefic planets, this can lead to alcohol and drug abuse and a desire of escaping reality.

3. Mrigashira natives may face life events, associated with love betrayal, marriage problems, infidelity, and suicide. These people can fall in love with a married person and try to separate him/her from the spouse. Very often they have children before marriage or date a person with a child. The reason for that is again the mythology of the nakshatra.

4. Love nature, forests, gardens, especially animals.

5. Both Mrigashira and Rohini nakshatras love to enjoy life.

6. Mrigashira and Rohini are ruled by snakes, so here again we see the theme of sex, but with a small difference. Mrigashira is a female serpent, and the seduction will involve love. The Rohini nakshatra is more about pleasure and seduction, while Mrigashira is about seduction, pleasure and falling deeply in love.

7. Mrigashira natives should be careful with people with prominent Uttara Ashadha nakshatra – mongoose eats the serpent. This constellation may produce bisexual or neutral-gender people.

8. Mrigashira natives have beautiful faces, faces like magnificent deer (especially if they have Ascendant in Mrigashira). Women will like big eyebrows in men and prominent noses.

9. Mrigashira natives may love drawing the Moon

10.   Mrigashira natives love gems, perfumes, fragrances and smelling things. They have a strong sense of smell. If they go to a restaurant, first they will smell the food.

11.   Mrigashira natives can be gentle, restless, sensitive, fragile, emotional, and indecisive. They can have a poetic soul, enjoy beauty, and love singing. They can be attached to their earthly needs and have a craving for sensations, always searching for new horizons and freedom.

12.   Age 32 is an important year for Mrigashira natives – their life can change.

13.   I remember that one of my teachers said about this nakshatra that natives may find a partner during travel. This partner will be younger/youthful and most probably the relationship will fail and cause a big transformation for the Mrigashira person. I have never seen this with my clients, so if you are Mrigashira native and experienced such an event, please send me an email. I am still gathering information about nakshatras.

14.   Mrigashira natives have to go through many failed relationships before they find their partner. This comes from the myth of Parvati, who was searching for her perfect partner, and Shiva

Remedies

The best remedy for Mrigashira is to go to the wild nature – forests, rivers, mountains, or to have a statue or picture of beautiful deer. Please note that the deer's antlers must not be missing or broken.

Careers/Hobbies

Mrigashira nakshatra may produce professions (or hobbies) related to:

- Animals and plants (flora and fauna) – farmers, gardeners, forest workers, food-related jobs, etc.

- Fragrance and perfumes, the fashion industry, the jewelry industry

- Travel and transport,

- Professions related to some kind of land, ground, or territory, like real estate agents (deer are territorial animals)

- All kinds of arts- poets, writers, etc.

- Profession related to searching, researching, exploring

Example

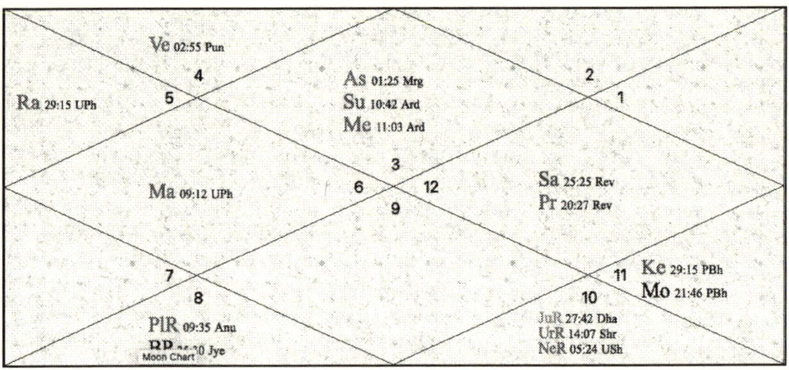

This is a chart of one of my clients – she has a Mrigashira Ascendant. She looks really beautiful like a deer – gentle and soft. She loves watching National Geographic movies about the wildlife in the forests, and jungles and the most interesting part is that she has a tapestry of deer in her vacation home

ARDRA

The Star of Sorrow

ZODIAC RANGE	6°40' GEMINI - 20°00' GEMINI
RULING PLANET	RAHU
DEITY	RUDRA
SYMBOL	TEARDROP OR DIAMOND
CASTE	BUTCHER
ANIMAL	FEMALE DOG
SOUNDS	KHU, GHAA, ING, CHHA
MAIN FIXED STARS	BETELGEUSE
PADAS	PADA 1- SAGITTARIUS PADA 2- CAPRICORN PADA 3- AQUARIUS PADA 4- PISCES
COLOR	GREEN
GENDER	FEMALE NAKSHATRA
KEY WORDS	SORROW, TEARS, GROWTH THROUGH PAIN, FRESH AND GREEN

Meaning

Ardra is the sixth nakshatra in the zodiac belt. It lies entirely in the zodiac sign Gemini, so Ardra is a mix of energy between Gemini, Mercury, and the ruler of this constellation -Rahu. What is Rahu? Rahu is one of the most interesting planets in Vedic Astrology. Rahu and Ketu are one demon[2] - Rahu is the head (without body), and Ketu is the body (without head). Ketu is your past, Rahu is your future, your mission on the planet Earth. Rahu is associated with desires, ambitions, and obsessions – Rahu wants everything material, it wants to achieve the impossible. It is connected to manipulations, illusions, foreigners, aerospace, and nuclear power. Rahu can make you successful and rich, but you have to pay the price! Ardra is the other difficult, heavy nakshatra, together with Bharani. Rahu nakshatras are always magnetizing, different and futuristic.

Ardra means "The moist one", "The green", and "The fresh". The symbol of the constellation is a teardrop or diamond. Some astrologers say the symbol can be the head of a human/skull. The teardrop indicates that Ardra people will have to face in their life sorrow and tears. Tears clean the soul and the eyes. They are related to water, moisture, and morning dew, so they bring freshness- water makes the grass green and alive! Through tears, the Ardra natives transform into diamonds! As you know, the diamond is created with heat and pressure, the same is with the Ardra people. There can be many life storms, which will produce an incredible glowing successful personality. You need the rain, to see the rainbow, right? The head is associated with the intellect and mind. The animal is a female dog. It is associated with Bhairava's dog- Shvan. Dogs are protective and loyal; they can be aggressive and wild.

---

2 Please refer to the creation story of Rahu and Ketu – Vedic Astrology Easy Simple, chapter 4

Deity

The Deity of Ardra is Rudra – the God of storms and destruction. Rudra is a form of Shiva. Rudra translates into the terrible, the howler. He destroys everything, he is the thunder god and God of wild animals. There are a lot of legends of Rudra in the scripts, and, I will be honest, they can be very confusing for a person, who is not part of Hindu culture, so I will try to simplify them for you.

<u>The Birth of Rudra:</u>

One of the myths related to the birth of Rudra is the one with Brahma. Brahma wanted to populate the world, so he started creating different beings. One day Brahma was so angry that the anger escaped from his eyebrows and took the form of Ardha-Nareshwara. This was a half man -half woman being. Brahma commanded the being to split into male and female forms. The being divided itself into a male called Rudra and a female form called Rudrani. After this, they split into another 11 parts. So, number 11 plays a role for Ardra natives and there is again a personality and gender duality in this nakshatra – half man, half woman.

Rudra is related to medicine, too- he is known as a great healer and in scripts he is illustrated with a medical pouch.

There is another popular legend about Rudra. It is related to Brahma and his lust for his daughter if you remember from Rohini nakshatra. The story has a different script in the different sources, so I will tell you the one my teachers told me. So, Gods, specifically Shiva, created Rudra in order to stop Brahma and protect the girl. Rudra hit one of the heads of Brahma and succeeded in his quest. However, the Gods were so ashamed of what they have done to the God of creation, that they abandoned Rudra and refused to accept him. Rudra was terrified by this unfair treatment and started howling and crying, creating storms. That's why Rudra is an outcast.

Another story is related to Mrigashira nakshatra – it says that Rudra was the form of Shiva that was married to Sita, the daughter of Daksha. When she burned into the sacred fire, Rudra was so angry that wanted revenge. Rudra created the giant Bhadravira. Rudra as Bhadravira charged the galaxies like a raging storm. The giant went to Daksha and according to some stories cut off his head. Rudra picked up the dead burned body of his beloved Sati and start crying.

Another story says that when Samudra Manthan (the churning of the Cosmic Ocean) happened, between the Devas and the Asuras, the first item to come forth was the poison named Halahal. Both the Gods and Demons were unable to consume the poison, and eventually, Shiva was the one who consumed it. His second wife Parvati held his neck so that the poison wouldn't go down to his body. Since then, Shiva's throat got blue-colored, and he got the nickname the Blue-throated one. So, Ardra people help and heal the world, they have a social cause.

Another myth is that Rudra was born without a name and started crying because he wanted a name. That's why Rudra translates as the howler, the screaming one.

Key Points

1. Ardra natives face very often sorrow, pain and tears in their life. They need to go through the storm and the rain in order to find happiness and success. You can see that these people cry a lot – when they listen to a song, watch a movie, or see injustice around them.

2. All Rahu nakshatras are eccentric and different, especially Ardra.

3. Ardra natives can be very angry and like screaming and shouting, or listening to singers with singing, that sounds like screaming for example something like the singing of Mariah Carey, Celine Dion, Christina Aguilera, etc.

4. Ardra natives are outcasts, they are loners. They are different from society and their family and feel that they are not accepted, that they are not wanted. They feel ignored and rejected. This comes from the mythology of Rudra.

5. Ardra natives love rain, storms, water, thunders, and lightning bolts. Great ideas can come to their minds if they meditate during a thunderstorm or rain.

6. Ardra natives are extremely intelligent. They have goals and mission, which will follow till the end – extremely successful and ambitious if they decide of course. Ardra people are very hard-working individuals. They want to have a "name" in society or at least in their professional circles. Unfortunately, these people most likely will succeed later in their life because the diamond needs time, heat, and pressure to become a diamond.

7. Ardra is associated with storms, bolts of lightning, electricity, new-age technology, and aerospace. It is related to cremation, too.

8. Ardra natives are wild, love dogs, and love eating meat or trying exotic meat. They like to chase and stalk and be like a hunter.

9. Ardra natives love science fiction and paranormal movies, movies for the wild animal life (especially the ones, involving dogs and

wolves) or fantasy movies with werewolves. Don't forget that Rudra is the God of wild animals

10.   Ardra people often interrupt others during conversation.

11.   They are great healers, too – any type of healing – from herbs to psychologists.

12.   Ardra natives are the most loyal friends, they are the most loyal spouses! They are extremely emotional and romantic people, but they will not show it to you, at least at the beginning. Remember the story of Rudra and Sita and their love. However, they are loyal enemies, too! Ardra native's actions can cause torment or pain to others.

13.   Ardra people fight for justice, they have social causes, and they fight for the unprivileged people and the outcasts. This comes from the story of Rudra and Brahma.

14.   Ardra natives may have tattoos on their arms.

15.   Ardra people love music, the occult, mysticism

16.   Number 11 plays a role in their life– there may be an event when they are 11 years old that will change their life or at least will be important for them.

17.   Ardra natives may have problems with their father -again due to the mythology of Rudra. There could be issues of abandonment or betrayal in the family.

18.   Ardra people can be obsessive, and they can "lose their head". You remember that Rudra was cutting off a lot of heads in mythology, so here

the natives can lose their mind, get obsessed with something or more literally hit their head, injured it somehow. They have to be careful with their throat, too

19. Ardra people love the green color, fresh grass, and mornings after rain. They may have specific eyebrows.

20. Ardra native can be critical, complaining, and ungrateful. They should learn how to be grateful in this life !!! There can be suicidal tendencies and addiction, too

21. Ardra natives transform and change a lot – they look for new growth by eliminating of old.

Remedies

The best remedy for Ardra natives is to have a dog, go in the wild, watch the rain outside, scream, and cry. Another good remedy is to practice gratitude.

You have to be careful not to have any broken electricity devices in your home – this will bring you bad luck.

Careers/Hobbies

Ardra nakshatra may produce professions (or hobbies) related to:

- Electricity and electronics - Computer Software Developers, Electricians, Electronic and Computer Industry, Sound Engineers and Technicians, Electronic Music, Computer Game Designers, 3D, and Virtual Reality Experts, Film Industry.

- Wild animals and weather

- Professions related to unprivileged people

- Medicine and healing

- Professions related to fantasy, fiction, space, cosmos

- Professions, related to communication, thinking or use of the hands

- Professions related to creating and destroying

Example

Famous people with Ardra nakshatra are Albert Einstein, Cher, and Princess Diana.

Cher is an example of eliminating the old through her ever-changing external appearance – she is always new, green, and fresh like Ardra. What is interesting is that the biggest music hit she had is "Believe", in which vocals are done with Auto-tune processor – a special electronic device, creating a computerized- robotic effect of the voice, which is typical Ardra manifestation.

PUNARVASU

The Star of Renewal

ZODIAC RANGE	20°00' GEMINI - 3°20' CANCER
RULING PLANET	JUPITER
DEITY	ADITI
SYMBOL	BOW / QUIVER OF ARROWS
CASTE	VAISHYA
ANIMAL	FEMALE CAT
SOUNDS	KAY, KHO, HAA, HEE
MAIN FIXED STARS	CASTOR POLLUX
PADAS	PADA 1- ARIES PADA 2- TAURUS PADA 3- GEMINI PADA 4- CANCER
COLOR	LEAD
GENDER	MALE NAKSHATRA
KEY WORDS	ABUNDANCE, WEALTH, TRAVELLING, REPEATING AGAIN AND AGAIN, RETURNING

Meaning

Punarvasu is the seventh nakshatra in the zodiac belt. It overlaps two zodiac signs- most of the nakshatra is in Gemini and a small part in Cancer. So, Punarvasu is a mixture of the energies of Gemini, Mercury, and the constellation's ruler Jupiter on the first side, and energies of Cancer, its ruler Moon and again Jupiter on the second side. The combination of Mercurian and Jupiterian energies may produce great intellectuals, thinkers. Jupiter and Moon are great friends, and in Cancer's part, they may produce great guardians and protectors.

What is Cancer? Cancer is associated with the mother, home, homeland, inner peace, and happiness. Cancer is warm, emotional, and sensitive. What is Jupiter? Jupiter is the Guru, the teacher. It is associated with religion, spirituality, wisdom, faith, belief system, money, luck, long-distance travelling, foreign lands, and expansion.

Punarvasu means "again prosperous", "wealthy again", or "return of the light". Punar means "return", and Vasu means "light, gem". The symbol of this nakshatra is a bow or a quiver with arrows. Arrows generally are associated with goals, targets, desires, and ambitions. The bow is a symbol of striving for something, aiming at something. That's why Punarvasu people should have goals and strive to achieve them. Bows and arrows are associated with moving, going on a mission and searching. The animal is a female cat. Cats are associated with wisdom, occult and mysticism, protection of their children and territory – they are mystical creatures.

Deity

The Deity of Punarvasu is **Aditi**- the Goddess of abundance, the mother of the 12 Sun Gods, called Adityas – Ansh, Aryaman, Bhaga, Dhatri, Tvashtar,

Mitra, Pushan, Savitar, Surya, Varuna, Vamana, Indra – most of them are deities of other nakshatras. Aditi means "unbounded". She is the goddess who is said to be the mother of all godly beings in the Universe. She is the universal mother, a personification of the infinite. Aditi is a space and is mentioned in Rig Veda as a repeating pattern (fractal) – God created Aditi and Aditi created God – this is related to reincarnation, rebirth. It is said that Vishnu reincarnated through Aditi 7 times. There is one interesting myth about Aditi and her sister Diti. Aditi is associated with the undivided, of the whole, mother of the Gods, while her sister, Diti, whose name means "divided" is the mother of the anti-gods, demons, the bounded space. According to Hindu philosophy, it is godly to unite and demonical to divide and separate. Another legend says that Aditi was fearful of the children of Diti and sent her child to destroy Diti's first child in her womb. Then Diti cursed Aditi that her children will repeatedly lose their kingdom to her children. That's why there is a constant fight between Gods and demons. Again, we see a repeating theme here.

Aditi is the goddess that grants abundance, and this is the reason that this nakshatra is one of the most beneficial.

Aditi and Maha Bali

One of the most popular myths associated with Aditi is the one with the demon Maha Bali (or only Bali). So, this demon conquered all the worlds, and the Gods lost their power. Aditi requested her husband to give her a son that can help God. Aditi gave birth to the reincarnation of Vishnu, who transformed into a beautiful child, named Vanama. The boy went to Maha Bali. When Vanama entered the room, everyone was amazed by the beauty of the boy, even the demon. Vanama was offered by Maha Bali to choose everything the boy wants – wealth and pleasures. The boy told the demon that he doesn't want wealth, he wants land that he can claim in three steps. Maha Bali was surprised but decided to give him what Vanama requested. Shukra (deity of Venus) tried to prevent this and told the demon that this is not a boy, but God Vishnu, but it was too late. Vanama transformed into Vishnu and conquered the world again in 3 steps, saving Gods.

<u>Lord Rama</u>

Lord Rama is associated with Punarvasu. Lord Rama is the seventh incarnation of Vishnu. He was exiled from his kingdom into the forest for 14 years by his stepmother and travelled around the world, living a humble life, helping other people, and saving them from demons. When his wife was kidnapped by a demon, he went to search for her. Together with Hanuman he defeated the demon, rescued his wife, and turned back to his kingdom. I am telling this story because it represents one important trait of Punarvasu natives – wherever they go, they turn back to their homeland.

Key Points

1. Punarvasu is a nakshatra ruled by Jupiter and it is more heavy nakshatra. Of course, it gives abundance, wealth, and prosperity, but natives should fight for them

2. Punarvasu people love to travel, some of them love traveling alone, but they always keep their homeland in their hearts and return back, like Lord Rama. They may feel exiled. It is possible that when they travel, they may take things from their home, so they can feel as though they are in their place. They love their home.

3. These people may be confused at the beginning of their life, and they may not know what to do. Just

like Rama had to leave his kingdom, the natives of this nakshatra find themselves somehow lost in their life. They may just want to do backpacking across the world, sleep on the floor, in hostels, eat whatever they can, and experience the world.

4. Punarvasu natives are honorable and will work for others, for the welfare of others and for nature.

5. Punarvasu natives have someone who is something like a brother figure for them, who is supporting and helping them, and who is deeply devoted to them– they can give their life for him.

6. Punarvasu people often will need to go far away to a different country to find their spouse.

7. Punarvasu people love to have goals, targets. They may love arrows or archery, going hunting, or fishing, depending on the planets that are placed in this nakshatra.

8. Punarvasu boyfriend/ girlfriend may be seduced by a third person

9. Punarvasu nakshatra is part of the merchant caste, so these natives are really good businessmen, they love doing business, especially in the field of real estate, lands, hotels, and resorts. This comes from the mythology.

10. Punarvasu means "return of the light" – these people will have to do things repeatedly. Most often, they will fail the first time and succeed the second time, after learning the lesson. So, if you have prominent Punarvasu in your natal chart – **don't give up**, if you can't make it the first time, always try again !!!! You will succeed the second time if you learn the lesson of course. There are constantly repeating patterns here – what I mean is you get something, then you lose it, then you get it back – the return of the light, wealthy again. You

can have a fortune, then lose it, then turn it back – you can see a lot of stories from the type -riches to rags and again rags to riches.

11.   There is a reincarnation theme here, constant rebirth! No matter how dark the hour is for these people, they always rise and come back to the status of king.

12.   Punarvasu are great communicators; inspirational speakers and they can control the crowd. Punarvasu natives excel in arts like poetry and writing. All these come from myths related to Lord Rama.

13.   If the 5th Lord is associated with Punarvasu, these people may have miscarriages. They can have twins, too- especially in the 3rd pada. It is believed that you can have more male children in this constellation.

14.   They are not good at taking feedback or criticism, they like being treated like royalty.

15.   If they are worried, often chew their nails

16.   Number 3 plays an important role for these natives – they may have 3 houses, 3 lands, or have to do things 3 times.

17.   Aditi is associated with virtues and strives to act nobly, so Punarvasu natives are noble, truthful, and respectful people. The mother plays an important role here – even they can become something like a mother figure that loves all her children. They can be very nurturing and caring

18.   Punarvasu natives love technology, especially sophisticated type electronics. They are people who love working with computers.

19. Punarvasu natives are supposed to be good with languages and will be well-educated and prosperous.

20. Punarvasu natives may suffer from dental issues and pain in their hands and feet. Due to mythology, they can lose money or property from in-laws.

21. Due to mythology, these natives may face marriage problems and difficulties, but the love between the spouses will win (if there is no bad planetary influence). It is said that Rama is the incarnation of the perfect man and his wife Sita-the perfect woman. Just to add here, if your 7th lord is in Punarvasu, most likely you will have 2 marriages or you will remarry your spouse.

22. Number 14 may play an important role in the life of these natives.

Remedies

The best remedy for this nakshatra is to have a female cat or statue of a cat or decorative arrows/a bow. Other things are to learn new languages, helping foreigners, and writing poems and mantras.

Careers/Hobbies

Punarvasu nakshatra may produce professions (or hobbies) related to:

- Trade and sales,

- Real estate, tourism and travelling

- Writing and speaking, communication, languages

- Homeland and lands, the earth itself

- Gurus, teachers, philosophers, preachers, monks

- Professions associated with science, knowledge, and education.

Example

Famous people with prominent Punarvasu nakshatra are Bill Gates, Robert De Niro, and Arnold Schwarzenegger.

Donald Trump has his Venus and Saturn in Punarvasu and maybe this is the reason that he is dealing with real estate and hotels and had multiple marriages. Furthermore, Donald Trump filed 4-5 bankruptcies in his life and always managed to stay ahead of the game. He attempted to run for president in the year 2012 and failed, but the second time, in 2016, he succeeded and became the president of the USA.

That is why I always say to my clients with Punarvasu nakshatra to try a second time!

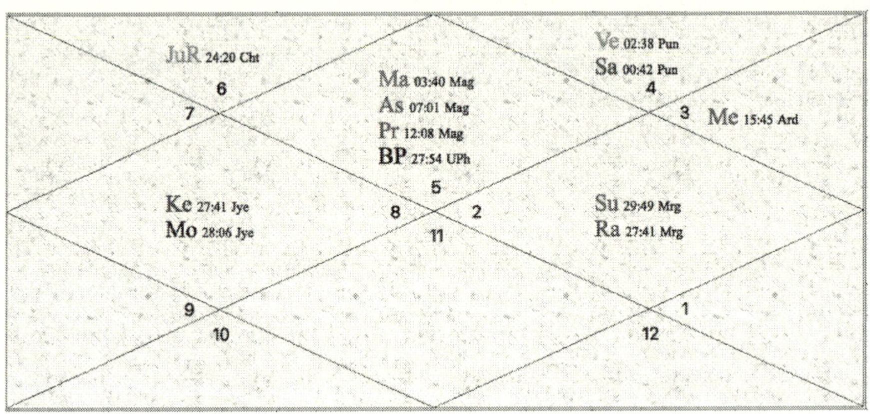

PUSHYA

The Star of Nourishment

ZODIAC RANGE	3°20' CANCER - 16°40' CANCER
RULING PLANET	SATURN
DEITY	BRIHASPATI
SYMBOL	UDDER OF A COW/FLOWER
CASTE	WARRIOR
ANIMAL	MALE GOAT/SHEEP
SOUNDS	HOO, HAY, HO, DA
MAIN FIXED STARS	THETA CANCRI, GAMMA CANCRI, ETA CANCRI
PADAS	PADA 1- LEO PADA 2- VIRGO PADA 3- LIBRA PADA 4- SCORPIO
COLOR	BLACKISH RED
GENDER	MALE NAKSHATRA
KEY WORDS	PROSPERITY, NOURISHING, EXPANSION, POPULARITY

Meaning

Pushya is the eighth nakshatra in the zodiac belt. It lies entirely in the zodiac sign Cancer. This constellation is a mix of the energies of the Cancer, its ruler the Moon and Saturn, which is the ruler of the nakshatra, together with Jupiter. Although Saturn is said to be a malefic planet, associated with sorrow, restrictions, delays, setbacks, organization, karmic lessons and events, it actually makes Pushya one of the most auspicious and fortunate nakshatras. Facing the karmic lessons and through hard work and discipline, Pushya natives can reach heights in life.

Pushya means "to nourish" or "the nourisher" – the main aim apart from nourishing is to protect, preserve, and strengthen. The symbol of this nakshatra is a cow's udder or a flower. The udder is associated with the ability to feed, nourish, and nurture. Cows are sacred animals in Hindu culture. They symbolize the mother, food, productivity, and fertility. The other symbol – a flower- is associated not only with beauty but with the ability of one person to grow and blossom like a flower, through nourishment and care. The animal is a ram/ male goat, which makes this nakshatra adaptable, clever, and productive.

Deity

The ruling deity of Pushya is **Brihaspati**- the lord of sacred speech and prayers. According to the Vedic scripts Shiva made Brihaspati into the planet Jupiter. This is the reason why Pushya has a strong influence not only by Saturn, its ruler but by Jupiter and everything it signifies. When you think of Pushya, you can think of Jupiter and its qualities. Jupiter and Saturn make the nakshatra very prosperous. Pushya nakshatra is where Jupiter is exalted.

Brihaspati is the Guru, the priest, and the advisor of the Gods. Brihaspati has the awareness of ego; he is the originator of the wisdom. The rituals, spirituality, and education play a crucial role in this nakshatra. The Guru brings happiness to the homes. Brihaspati is the one who advises Gods on their duties and rituals. He is said to give fortune, children, and expansion. He is associated with books and politics, Vedic teachings, too.

Shukra and Brihaspati

One of the myths linked to the Pushya deity is the one with Shukra (Venus). Brihaspati was a brilliant student, and his classmate Shukra considered him a rival. Later on, Brihaspati became the guru of the gods and Shukra – the guru of demons. This is the reason why Venus and Jupiter have animosity in astrology. So, if you see Jupiter and Venus aspecting each other in someone's chart, you should always take into consideration that there will be some kind of conflict there – a clash between the Guru of Gods and the Guru of Demons.

Shani and Brihaspati

Another difficult planetarian relationship can be explained by the myth of Brihaspati and Shani (which is Saturn). According to Hindu mythology, Brihaspati refused to educate Shani and be his Guru. Saturn was forced to go to Shukra, who became his teacher. This is the reason why Shani and Shukra (Saturn and Venus) are in the same planetary camp and Saturn is a friend of Venus, not a friend of Jupiter.

Indra and Brihaspati

This myth is associated with the punishment of Indra, the king of the Gods. Brihaspati went to Indra, but Indra didn't pay attention to the Guru and proceeded with his luxurious activities. Brihaspati felt neglected, left the place, and decided to punish Indra. Indra suddenly realized his mistake and went to apologize, but Brihaspati became invisible and could not be found. The demons heard that the Gods are without their Guru, attacked them, and almost defeated them. So, the lesson here is that everyone should pay respect to knowledge, teachings, and wisdom, because without them – the world cannot survive.

Tara and Brihaspati

Brihaspati was married to Tara, but he didn't pay attention to his wife – he was too busy working, doing ceremonies, and advising the Gods. She felt neglected and fell in love with Chandra. After a brief conflict, Gods helped Brihaspati, so Tara had to turn back to him again, but she was already pregnant with Buddha (Mercury). Brihaspati accepted her child as his own.

Another legend says that Brihaspati is the son of Angiras and Shraddha. They prayed to Lord Agni for a child by performing fire rituals and Agni blessed them with a son. They called him Brihaspati. He was an intelligent, wise, brilliant thinker and student. He became the greatest scholar. His mother's name means faith and trust, so it is said that the God comes from the faith.

Key Points

1. Pushya natives can be highly disciplined, organized, and hard-working. They can be very successful and stand out in their personal and professional life. This is due to Saturn's influence.

2. Pushya nakshatra is one of the most prosperous nakshatras and gives abundance to their natives if there are no afflicted planets there. It is recommended always to start a new business on the day when Moon is transiting the Pushya constellation. Of course, it depends on the whole chart again.

3. Pushya natives can be well-educated, clever, wise, compassionate, kind, joyful and optimistic. Education, knowledge, and intellect are important! If you have prominent Pushya nakshatra you have to pay attention to your intellectual development.

4. Pushya natives love to nourish/feed other people, love cooking, and love family meals. The breast will be a special part of their body – you may have some kind of a mark, spot of the breast or chest. Many times, women with Pushya have plastic surgeries on their breasts or there is something in their life, associated with breasts or breastfeeding.

5. Pushya people most probably will have a delay in their success – their life will start growing after they become 32 years old. Till then, they will need to follow the Saturn karmic rules. Age 15/ 16 can be crucial for them.

6. Pushya people may love milk and milk products, they may have strong digestive systems.

7. Pushya people can be good advisers, teachers, preachers, scholars, motivational, life and business coaches, and mentors. They can be great generals and politicians, too.

8. Pushya natives love their homeland, and they are big patriots- many times you can see the flag of their country somewhere in their home.

9. Pushya natives can face a lot of rivalry and jealousy in their life due to the Shukra and Brihaspati myth.

10. Pushya natives may be working too much and neglecting the other fields of their life, so they have to find the right balance.

11. Pushya natives have to be careful how and what they speak – their words can become reality. Praying is important. Brihaspati is the lord of the prayers, so if you are in trouble, you should pray, and you will be heard! It is recommended to have your rituals, too. You should never insult a teacher or guru.

12. Pushya natives may get married to a person with a child or their spouse can be seduced by others. This is a result of the myth of Tara and Brihaspati.

13. Pushya people may love fragrances and perfumes. They may love fire rituals, and barbeques, too

14. Pushya people can be very influential in their professional circles and society. They can become role models.

15. These natives can have 2 homes, 2 lands.

16. Pushya people may have an interest in magic and tantra. Angiras taught Brihaspati the magical spells of Atharvaveda.

17. Venus doesn't feel very happy in Pushya nakshatra and sometimes it can create difficult marriages or cheating of the spouse. Moon does not feel very comfortable in the Pada of the Scorpio -13°20' -16°40' Cancer.

18. Pushya natives will always bring things from their past to show what they had to endure during that time.

19. Pushya natives are known to have vibrating muscles, twinkling in their fingers and sometimes they cannot control the movement of their hands (as though they are getting cerebral palsy). This usually occurs in a panic situation.

Remedies

The best remedy for this nakshatra is to pay attention to your education and intellectual development. Praying is a way to strengthen this constellation or having/ watching cows, having fire rituals, too. It is recommended to have a guru or advisor.

Careers/Hobbies

Pushya nakshatra may produce professions (or hobbies) related to:

- Food and cooking – all kinds of professions in the food industry, milk industry, restaurants and bar business, food and drinks merchants, caterers, etc.

- Nourishment and nurturing – professions related to the hospitality industry, taking care of people like nurses, caregivers at old age homes, NGOs, supporting the sick and dying, charitable organizations, etc.

- Education and knowledge – teachers, scholars, etc.

- Spirituality, religion, magic – priests, nuns, gurus, tantra specialists.

- Advising and coaching

- Politics and Government of the Homeland

- The land itself – geologists, real estate agents, etc.

Example

I will give you an example of one of my clients, who booked a career consultation with me. This is a typical Pushya native. This individual has Moon and Ascendant in Pushya. The first manifestation is her job -at the beginning of her career life, she was working in the field of real estate and after that working in the municipality of her hometown (governing the homeland). She has plastic surgery on her breasts – she was obsessed and wanted to have bigger breasts. The last manifestation of Pushya is that her spouse has a child from a previous marriage.

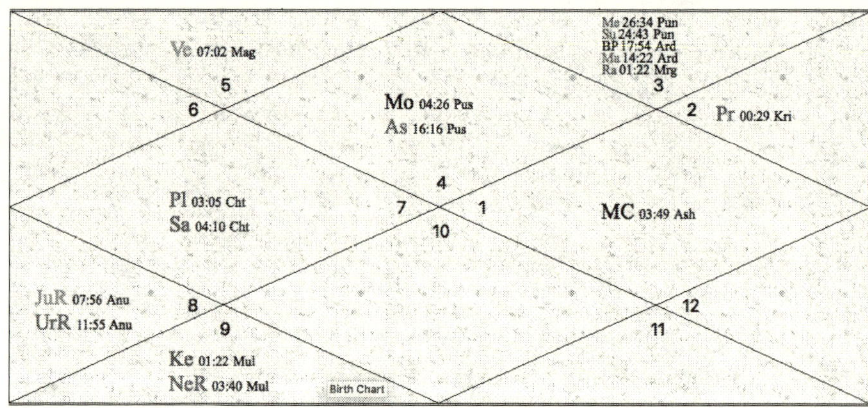

ASHLESHA

The Clinging Star

ZODIAC RANGE	16°40' CANCER - 30°00' CANCER
RULING PLANET	MERCURY
DEITY	NAGA, THE SERPENT KING
SYMBOL	A CURLED-UP SERPENT
CASTE	OUTCASTE
ANIMAL	MALE CAT
SOUNDS	DEE, DOO, DAY, DOH
MAIN FIXED STARS	EPSILON HYDRAE, DELTA HYDRAE, MU HYDRAE, RHO HYDRAE, SIGMA HYDRAE, ZETA HYDRAE
PADAS	PADA 1- SAGITTARIUS PADA 2- CAPRICORN PADA 3- AQUARIUS PADA 4- PISCES
COLOR	RED, BLACK, BLACKISH RED
GENDER	FEMALE NAKSHATRA
KEY WORDS	HYPNOTIZING, SEXUAL, CONTROVERSIAL, DECEIVING

Meaning

Ashlesha is the ninth nakshatra in the zodiac belt. It lies entirely in the zodiac sign of Cancer. Here, you feel the energies of Cancer, the Moon, and the ruler of this constellation- Mercury. You already learnt the myth about Chandra, Tara, and Buddha, so you know that Moon and Mercury are not friends in Vedic Astrology, which leads to more negative manifestations of the Mercurial energy. Ashlesha uses Mercurial negative traits like deception, selfishness, manipulation, and deceiving others to fulfil its own goals. This negative manifestation of Mercury makes Ashlesha very dangerous nakshatra, still, it is very powerful on a spiritual level.

Ashlesha means "embracing", or "clinging" and it is called the clinging star because it wants to embrace and entangle the object of their desire. The symbol is a coiled snake (serpent), which animal is associated with wisdom, occult, transformation, and change (through shedding their skin). Snakes can be deceptive, insincere, too. They are famous for their poison, which can kill, but in the right quantity, it can heal, too. Snakes are an important part of Hindu culture. The animal of this nakshatra is the male cat, which is again a symbol of cleverness, selfishness, and mysticism. The whole combination of symbols is proof that Ashlesha is a really difficult nakshatra with strong kundalini energy that is hard to handle. It has extremely strong esoteric significance.

Deity

The ruling deity of Ashlesha is the **Naga**, The Serpent King, who is half-snake, half-human. Nagas are the snakes, who have spiritual/occult powers- not just normal snakes- Naga is the divine serpent.

Nagas are the children of Sage Kasyapa and Kadru. Sage Kasyapa got married to 13 sisters and with each of the sisters, he produced different species of offspring. One of the sisters, Kadru, wanted many children and laid 1000 legs from which hatched different species of serpents. However, her sister Vinata wanted only 2 children, but powerful. From her eggs hatched Aruna and Garuda (Eagle King). Kadru got jealous that Vinata has so powerful children and decided to destroy them. She made a bet with Vinata and through the help of part of her children, succeeded to deceive her and win the bet. The other part of the Kadru's children refused to participate in this manipulation, and they became special species of Nagas. They are proof that not all nagas are deceptive and manipulative. So, Vinata's children become slaves to Kadru and her children. Garuda wanted freedom and asked the Nagas how he can be free, and they requested from him to bring them the Soma, the elixir of the Gods and he will be free. Garuda hated the snakes but wanted to be free and decided to trick the nagas. Together with Indra, they created a plan for how to take his freedom back. The king of Eagles took the Soma and gave it to the nagas. He was free from slavery. The moment he got his freedom, Indra came out of nowhere and took the elixir back, however, some drops splashed on the sharp grass. Nagas licked the grass, so they can drink the drops and become powerful, however, the sharp grass split their tongues in two, and that's why snakes have split tongues.

Nagas inhabit different dimension/realm, which is full of pleasures, enjoyment, and beauty; it is decorated with beautiful shedding jewels and splendid ornaments, surrounded by beautiful streams and lakes, fragrant perfumes, and music. Unlike other supernatural beings, snakes have always had a strong bond with the physical and tangible world. It is seen by some as either hoarding wealth or guarding it.

One of the most famous nagas in Hindu mythology are Vasuki, Shesha, and Kaliya. Vasuki is the King of the

Nagas. Some associate Vasuki with Rahu, the North Node of the Moon. Vasuki played an essential role in churning the ocean of milk. Lord Shiva wears Vasuki coiled around his neck. When the gods and demons needed to extract the essence of immortality from the ocean of milk, they wrap Vasuki around Mount Mandara and use him as a rope to churn the ocean.

In some traditions, the Nagas have been referred as a race of dragons.

Key Points

1. Ashlesha natives have strong kundalini energy, esoteric powers, and abilities. They are interested in the paranormal, tantra, occult and magic. They believe in mystical things in life.

2. Ashlesha natives have specific karma in this life – they will need to finish something, some pattern needs to be finalized, put the end of something. This karma may be related to different fields of their lives. Maybe you have a dysfunctional family, for example, and you are the one who will stop all the patterns that bring pain and trouble.

3. Ashlesha people can be hypnotizing and mesmerizing, they may have beautiful eyes. Sometimes they may look cold in their outer appearance.

4. Ashlesha natives can be very sexual and if there are malefic planets in this nakshatra, they can use sex to reach their goals. Ashlesha produces many bisexual people, people with sexual fetishes like BDSM, costumes, and sex toys. They may have issues with marriage and infidelity.

5. Ashlesha natives are interested in poisons, oils, pharmacy, chemicals, Ayurveda, and toxic liquids. They may have love or fear for snakes and other reptiles.

6. Ashlesha natives can be jealous, suspicious, cunning, manipulative, egocentric, and deceiving. The theme of tricking someone will be significant for them. They can be tricked, and they can trick and lie, too. Ashlesha people can be very cruel and speak cruel words that can destroy someone's ego. They can manifest all negative traits of Mercury.

7. Ashlesha natives may be able to hypnotize others and have an influence on the crowds. Good in selling things, good spiritual leaders, magnificent orators, and speakers. Good in learning languages.

8. Ashlesha natives love sleeping curled up like a snake. They may love eating eggs, too.

9. Ashlesha natives most often don't feel connected to this world, and they know that this is not their place. Very often they go to past life regressions to find the truth. They may face a paranormal event in their life or a spiritual transformation, a life metamorphosis, which can change their path.

10. People with nakshatras that are associated with snakes, very often have problems with their skin.

11. Ashlesha people may love jewelry, gems, beautiful ornaments, and perfumes and may have beautiful homes like the realm of the Nagas. They have connections both to the spiritual and material world.

12.   Ashlesha people can be good healers and doctors.

13.   Ashlesha natives have a deep connection to both the dark and bright sides of nature. They have the capacity to do both good and bad things. They may have an interest in psychology, astrology, and want to explore the hidden aspects of consciousness. They may have mental issues, worry, fear and issues with the nervous system. They may have unstable emotions, huge egos, and problems with forgiving.

14.   Ashlesha natives could be involved in illegal actions such as tax evasion and secret deals. Ashlesha natives like to live and work in seclusion. It is also seen they do things in secret; they may be very introverted.

15.   Ashlesha people can be very competitive and ambitious.

16.   Ashlesha and Uttara Bhadrapada are the most mysterious nakshatras. Ashlesha natives are natural psychics and have natural intuition within them, no matter whether they are bankers, actors, detectives, or occultists. Ashlesha natives know how to play mind games and dissect others without looking bad.

17.   Ashlesha natives are very much into the environment and environmental causes

18.   Transformation and change are important themes for these natives.

Remedies

The best remedy for this nakshatra is to have a clean and beautiful home or a cat, which is the ruling animal of Ashlesha. You can have hobbies in psychology, astrology or detoxicate your body often. Do not kill or hurt snakes and cats – this will bring bad luck in your life. Ashlesha is the clinging star, so maybe it is good to hug the one you love or go into nature and hug trees, so they can take the negative energy you have.

Careers/Hobbies

Ashlesha nakshatra may produce professions (or hobbies) related to:

- Healing and medicine – healers, surgeons, physicians, etc.

- Professions related to chemicals, poisons, oils, and drugs

- Professions related to occult, esoteric, psychology, transformation, astrology, and spirituality

- Professions related to secrecy and manipulation– spies, secret agents, investigators, etc.

- Professions associated with hypnotizing others, selling something to others.

- Professions related to snakes, reptiles, and other animals

- Professions related to jewels, gems, and decorating homes.

Example

I will give you an example of one of my clients, who booked horoscope reading with me. She has an Ascendant in Ashlesha. She had some issues with dysfunctional family patterns that she had to stop in order to heal. Strangely, she loves snakes and watching movies with snakes, for example, the movie Anaconda.

She even has a ring in the form of a snake. She has some sexual addictions and fetishes, which I am not going to mention here, but definitely they are manifestations of Ashlesha. She has issues with the skin – dermatitis- and needs to put in some special bio-oils to heal it.

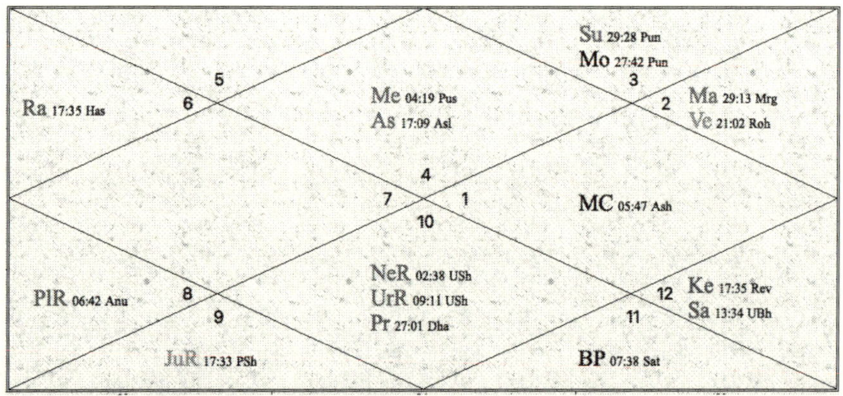

Ashlesha is the last nakshatra from the first circle of nakshatras. All 27 nakshatras are divided into 3 main circles by 9 constellations. Each circle includes a fire, an earth, an air and a water zodiac sign and the rulers of the nakshatras have the same order – the first nakshatra of each circle will be always ruled by Ketu and the last by Mercury.

The first 9 are associated with Rajas energy – the energy to create, the second circle is linked to Tamas energy – the energy to destroy, and the third circle of 9 nakshatras are linked to Sattva energy – the energy to maintain.

Rajas is associated with activity, Tamas with the material world and Sattva with the liberation from the material world- spirituality.

MAGHA

The Star of Power

ZODIAC RANGE	00°00' LEO - 13°20' LEO
RULING PLANET	KETU
DEITY	PITRIS, THE DIVINE FOREFATHERS
SYMBOL	CROWN/THRONE
CASTE	SHUDRA
ANIMAL	MALE RAT
SOUNDS	MAA, MEE, MOO, MAY
MAIN FIXED STARS	REGULUS
PADAS	PADA 1- ARIES PADA 2- TAURUS PADA 3- GEMINI PADA 4- CANCER
COLOR	CREAM
GENDER	FEMALE NAKSHATRA
KEY WORDS	ROYAL, AMBITIOUS, SUCCESS TRADITIONS, ANCESTORS

Meaning

Magha is the tenth nakshatra in the zodiac belt. It lies entirely in the zodiac sign Leo. It is a mixture of the creative fire energy of Leo, its ruler -The Sun, and the ruler of the constellation- Ketu.

What is Leo? Leo is related to the king, children, and big families. Leo is proud, royal, the center of attention, creative, artistic, and romantic. Leo rules art, media, cinema, love and romance, celebrities, politicians, and education. Leo is linked to your past life deeds, too. In Magha nakshatra, Ketu is associated mostly with our past life karma, ancestors and what you bring from your ancestors. Magha is really a unique combination between the Sun and Ketu that put the focus on the family and all your kindred.

Magha means "mighty" or "the great one". This tells us that the constellation can make its natives great and powerful. The symbol is a crown or a throne, which we associate with royalty, authority, power, status, honor, and success. The animal of the nakshatra is the male rat. Rats are clever animals, with big families and they can be very destructive, too. Often the animal is related to Vahana – the rat that Ganesha rides. Vahana was a demon that Ganesha transformed into a rat and used him as a riding vehicle. This tells us that in Magha nakshatra there is tamas energy that we should handle carefully to take the best of life.

One of the most auspicious fixed stars lies at the heart of Magha and Leo's zodiac sign – Regulus. Regulus or Alpha Leonis is placed at around 5° of Leo (Sidereal calculation system). It is called "the little king" and it is said that gives fame, power, and prosperity and makes the natives, who have prominent planets around this degree, like kings. You can check if you have any point/planet that is placed around 5° of Leo, just keep in mind that it has to be close conjunction – maximum +/-

2° - so you should check the span between 3° till 7° of Leo. The other factor that you need to take into consideration is that the different planets give different results when they are placed in Leo. If you have an Ascendant, Moon or Sun influenced by Regulus, for sure you can get very successful, powerful, and popular, however, if you have Saturn – the effect will be totally different. Again, we need to check the whole natal horoscope.

Deity

The ruling deity of Magha is **Pitris**, the forefather of humanity, the ancestors. Traditions, family values and the whole lineage play crucial roles in this nakshatra. The forefathers guide their children and support them. Magha bestows gifts from our ancestors like inheritance of qualities, DNA, and fortune. Forefathers represent the collective consciousness that has been carried forward from generation to generation. It is believed that Magha is the constellation, where our ancestors wait to reincarnate back with their families on Earth.

Pitris are the divine beings between the original offspring of Brahma and the Gods, humans, and animals. There are forefathers of the non-human, called Devas Pitris, and the human, called Manushya Pitris. The main aim of the Pitris is to bring peace and prosperity to their descendants – they keep the roots alive.

Key Points

1. Magha natives should always honor their departed ancestors and keep their roots and family values alive.

2. Magha natives can become very rich, successful, powerful and have a royal status in society. They can be very ambitious, too.

3. Magha people have a strong connection with their ancestors and have some kind of karma that they need to finish here on this Earth. This karma can be related to the life and deeds of their departed relatives or from their own past life.

4. Magha natives love sex, and they can have a lot of children and create big families. They love family gatherings, family traditions and the real home environment.

5. Magha people are connected to the land of their ancestors – they want to have their own lands and properties. My teachers told me that if you have Mars in Magha, you can get real estate, Moon and Jupiter- land with crops, Venus – land in the city, Saturn – bare land. If you have Sun in Magha, you may want to create a temple, however, I could not conclusively confirm with my horoscope consultations if this property theory is correct and corresponds to real life.

6. These people are big patriots and love their home country and national heroes. They may have the flag of their country put on the wall or the desk. These are the people who always celebrate their national holidays.

7. Magha natives always think about death and life after death. They have an interest in the occult.

8. Magha natives want to present themselves in a kingly, royal manner, they want to show off. When they have children, they will show off them or their ancestors. At the beginning of

their life, they can have a big ego and speak only about themselves.

9. Magha natives are generous and loyal people.

10. Magha natives want power, recognition, and success. However, they should not be overly attached to power, because they will fail in this way. They should serve society using their position and authority.

11. Magha people are connected to the past and want to know their origin and what is their family tree. They are interested in researching their lineage or family genealogy. Very often you will see them having genetic tests in order to understand where they come from.

12. Magha people are interested in history, biographies, military sagas, documentaries and ancient civilizations like the Greeks, Egyptians, Romans, Aztecs, and Mayans. They may love antiques and collecting old objects.

13. Magha natives can benefit from legacies, estates and properties, insurance, and inheritance. They can have their own family business or participate in the business of their family and relatives.

14. If there are malefic aspects, there could be problems due to ancestors.

15. Magha natives may have high political or government positions, they may be volunteering in political parties or elections. They would like to be part of the aristocracy and the elite.

Remedies

The best remedy for this nakshatra is to have beautiful chairs. Especially if you want to succeed in life, you should have a chair like a throne. If you have broken chairs in your home, you should fix them immediately. Another remedy is always to honor your ancestors and your family and participate in different causes, related to your homeland.

Magha people are connected with their departed loved ones and if you are in trouble and pain, you can always ask them for help and assistance.

Careers/Hobbies

Magha nakshatra may produce professions (or hobbies) related to:

- Government, management, politics, and any type of professions linked to authority and power – CEOs, kings, politicians, managers of companies, etc.

- History and the past of humankind – like archaeologists, historians, antique collectors, museum workers, etc.

- Family, traditions, genealogy

- Professions related to the land, properties, and homeland.

- Family-owned businesses

- Lawyers and judges

- Occult and mysticism – this is influenced by Ketu.

- Professions associated with art and media

Example

I will give you an example of one of my clients, who booked yearly horoscope reading with me. She has an Ascendant in Magha.

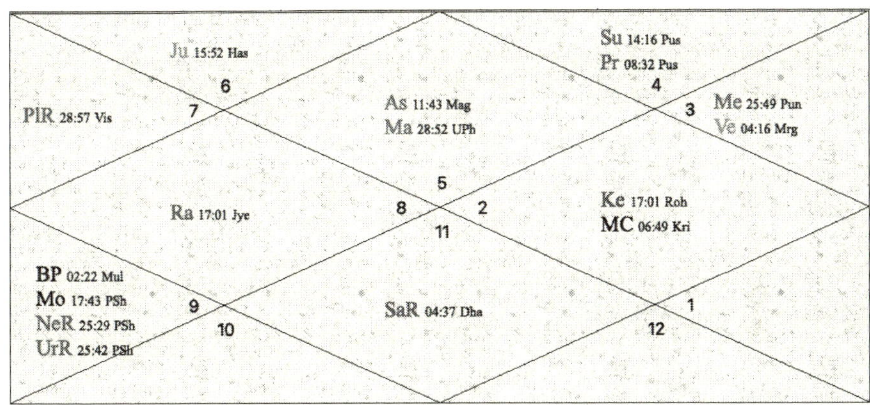

This client has a big family and although she lives abroad, she loves her homeland. She had made a genetic test to find her origin and learn more about her family tree.   She loves watching movies about the history of Europe and loves ancient Greek culture. She works in the media field.

You see how all nakshatras leave their prints on the human life. Nakshatras really give us explanation for our desires and personal traits.

PURVA PHALGUNI

The Fruit of the Tree

ZODIAC RANGE	13°20' LEO - 26°40' LEO
RULING PLANET	VENUS
DEITY	BHAGA
SYMBOL	THE FRONT PART OF A BED
CASTE	PRIEST
ANIMAL	FEMALE RAT
SOUNDS	MO, TAA, TEE, TOO
MAIN FIXED STARS	DELTA LEONIS THETA LEONIS
PADAS	PADA 1- LEO PADA 2- VIRGO PADA 3- LIBRA PADA 4- SCORPIO
COLOR	LIGHT BROWN
GENDER	FEMALE NAKSHATRA
KEY WORDS	LOVE, SEX, CREATIVITY, PROSPERITY

Meaning

Purva Phalguni is the eleventh nakshatra in the zodiac belt. It lies entirely in the zodiac sign Leo. Purva Phalguni is a mixture of the creative energy of Leo, the Sun and Venus, which is the ruler of this nakshatra. Key words are sex, love, and creativity. An important part is to create a family or the process of creating in general – you can create a child, an idea, art, or something else. Venus brings to this nakshatra affinity to beauty and physical appearance.

Purva Phalguni means "the former reddish one" or "the little fig tree". Purva stands for first, former, Phal stands for fruit, and Gunin is auspicious. It is the fruit of your good deeds. Purva Phalguni and Uttara Phalguni are two constellations, which are consisted of four stars that look like a bed in the sky. Purva is the front part of the bed, and Uttara is the back part of the bed. This tells us that their traits are similar. Purva Phalguni's bed is more about afternoon relaxation, rather than a night's sleep. It is associated with having rest and fun after fulfilling your tasks, with enjoyment and comfort. This nakshatra is all about enjoying life. The animal is a female rat, the same animal as Magha nakshatra. We associate it with cleverness, big families, and destructive energy, too. However here the focus is procreation. Female rats can give birth to a lot of mice, and this makes the nakshatra extremely fruitful and sex-oriented. I know from my Vedic teachers that Purva and Uttara Phalguni are the nakshatras associated a lot with porn actors.

For example, you can check the chart of Kim Kardashian

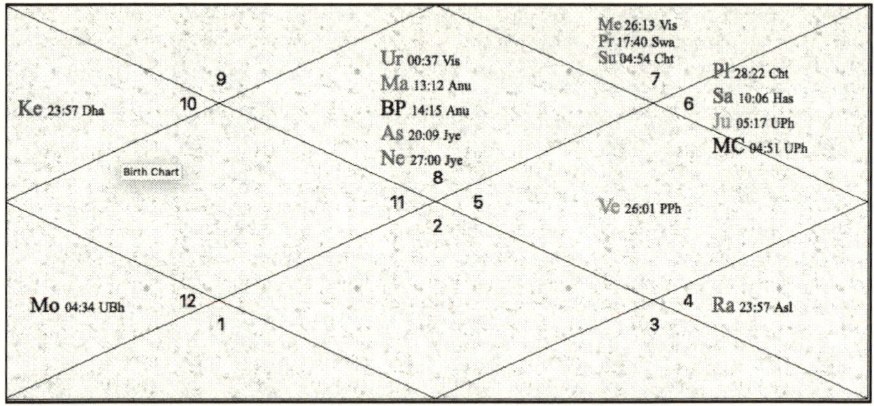

She has Venus in the tenth house in Purva Phalguni. The tenth house is associated with fame and status, Venus with sex, sexuality, and beauty, and it is placed in its own nakshatra- Purva Phalguni. This is the reason why she got famous for her sex tape and her beauty and body. You can check my YouTube channel - Astrology Coaching by Anatoly – I have a special video about Kim Kardashian.

Purva Phalguni is the nakshatra of the happy lovers and romance.

Deity

The ruling deity of Purva Phalguni is **Bhaga**, one of the Adityas – solar deities. Bhaga is the God of good fortune and luck. The deity indicates that the natives of this constellation will have the opportunity to achieve a lot in their life and get the golden fruits from the "little fig tree". Bhaga grants materialistic pleasures, achievements, and swealth; he is associated with inheritance, too. Bhaga and Aryaman, the deity of Uttara Phalguni, are said to bring prosperity, happiness, and happy marriages.

Bhaga is associated with the womb, children, creation, enjoyment, relaxation, and sexual passion.

One of the myths associated with Bhaga is related to Sage Daksha and Shiva. When the daughter of Daksha, Sati died in the sacred fire, Shiva came for revenge. Bhaga was one of the main priests at the ceremony and supposedly winked at Shiva, which made Shiva very angry. Shiva poked the eyes of Bhaga and made him blind. That's why it is said that Bhaga gives wealth, fame, and status blindly – it gives them to everyone, without any precautions or prejudices. He is famous as "the giver". Of course, Shiva later turns back the eyesight to Bhaga.

Purva Phalguni is the nakshatra, where the Moon was placed when Shiva started his second marriage.

Key Points

1. Purva Phalguni natives are extremely sexual and attracted to beauty and physical appearance. Huge appetite for sex, lust, fame, status, and wealth. They want to be noticed. They want everything in a big manner- the best of everything.

2. Purva Phalguni people should be careful with their eyes and eyesight. Bhaga was blinded, so you should consider it – literally and figuratively. These people should keep an eye on all matters and don't trust anybody blindly. It is said that these natives will fall in love blindly at least once in their life and their hearts will be broken.

3. The theme of committing suicide plays a role here – they may think about suicide, especially after a breakup, or they can know people, who committed suicide.

4. Purva Phalguni people love a cozy atmosphere, love staying in bed, love comfort, material pleasure and luxury.

5. These people are extremely creative and talented – they can become great artists, musicians, and writers. All types of artistic, and creative professions, speaking and performing on stage or any other platforms can be seen here.

6. Purva Phalguni natives want to create a family, they are attached to children. It is said that if you have a prominent Purva Phalguni nakshatra, your life will excel after you get married.

7. Purva Phalguni may love eating salted food, sushi, or salmon. They may have a big appetite, and this can cause health problems. Purva Phalguni people may have a habit of either raising their eyebrows or winking with their eyes while talking. This comes from the myth of Bhaga and Shiva.

8. Purva Phalguni people may look youthful, beautiful, seducing, and attractive. They don't like to worry about things and to hurry. These natives like extremes – they can be like party animals, and the center of attention and suddenly become monks or spiritual people.

9. These natives may have an inheritance. They will have opportunities for achieving success, fortune, and fame.

10. Purva Phalguni people are very social- they can make friends and connections easily. They love recreation, relaxing, having fun, and enjoying life. They like weddings, matchmaking and everything related to this field.

11.   These people love art, media, the entertainment industry, and Hollywood.

12.   They can be very generous people and take part in different political or social causes.

13.   They should be careful with fire – there can be some accidents.

14.   Bhaga's obsession with the physical aspect of the world, often makes Purva Phalguni natives obsessed or concerned with their bodies. If there is malefic influence, this can create unhealthy body image issues and eating disorders.

15.   These people can be vain, jealous, and arrogant.

16.   Semen and the penis, as a symbol of creation and continuation of life, play a role in this constellation.

Remedies

The best remedy for this nakshatra is to have beautiful furniture and especially beds. If you have a broken bed or couch in your home, you should fix them immediately.

If you need to relax, it is good to have an afternoon sleep and rest. This will give you energy. Socializing and going out, and having fun is another remedy for Purva Phalguni natives.

Careers/Hobbies

Purva Phalguni nakshatra may produce professions (or hobbies) related to:

- Art, media, entertainment industry, show business and everything related to celebrities.

- Sex and sex appeal

- Fashion, jewelry, and beauty industry

- Matchmaking and weddings, social activities

- Family and children

- Professions related to luxury, leisure, and entertainment in general

- Diplomats and government officials,

- Wealth and inheritance.

Examples

Famous people with prominent Purva Phalguni nakshatra are Madonna, Raquel Welch, and John Travolta. This nakshatra may produce a lot of celebrities. Madonna is a typical manifestation of Purva Phalguni – sexy, provocative, and creative!

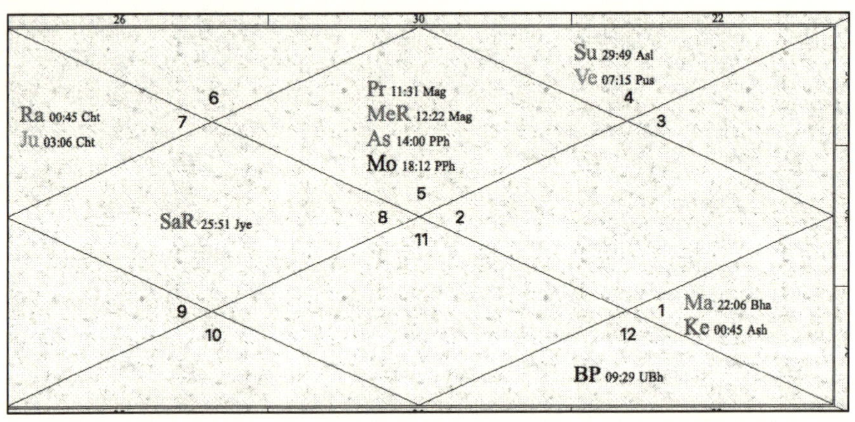

UTTARA PHALGUNI

The Star of Patronage

ZODIAC RANGE	26°40' LEO -10°00' VIRGO
RULING PLANET	SUN
DEITY	ARYAMAN
SYMBOL	THE BACK PART OF A BED
CASTE	WARRIOR
ANIMAL	BULL
SOUNDS	TAY, TOO, PAA, PEE
MAIN FIXED STARS	DENEBOLA
PADAS	PADA 1- SAGITTARIUS PADA 2- CAPRICORN PADA 3- AQUARIUS PADA 4- PISCES
COLOR	LIGHT BLUE
GENDER	FEMALE NAKSHATRA
KEY WORDS	LOVE, SEX, PROSPERITY, HELPFULNESS, KINDNESS

Meaning

Uttara Phalguni is the twelfth nakshatra in the zodiac belt. It overlaps two zodiac signs – starts at 26°40' Leo and ends at 10°00' Virgo. So, in the first part, this constellation is strongly influenced by the traits of the zodiac sign Leo and the Sun, which is both ruler of the sign and the nakshatra. On the other part, Uttara Phalguni is influenced by the energy of Virgo, Mercury and again Sun.

What is Virgo? Virgo is the sixth zodiac sign and is associated with health, healing, hard-working, dealing with conflicts, arguments, and social reforms. Virgo is critical, practical, detailed-oriented, and helpful. It is associated with the Prarabdha karma – past life karma that you cannot escape. Sun represents authority, strength and creates here great leaders, especially in the portion of the Leo. On the side of Virgo, the combination of the Sun and Mercury produce great thinkers and intellectuals. It can create leaders, too, but the focus here is the intellect and healing of society- not (only) the power and Ego.

Uttara Phalguni means "The latter Reddish one", or "The latter Fig tree" and has almost the same traits as Purva Phalguni with some differences, of course. All nakshatras, which have Purva and Uttara portions, have similar backgrounds. Purva Phalguni was the front part of a bed and Uttara Phalguni is the back part of a bed. Purva is associated with fun and relaxation after the work is done, while Uttara Phalguni is when you have already had your rest and now you are preparing for work again. Uttara Phalguni is more active and ambitious than Purva. Uttara is associated with someone, who is on the bed or couch, but thinking, writing, or doing some kind of activity, not just lying and relaxing. It is connected to the place or platform, where the Guru sits and teaches his students. That's why this nakshatra can produce great teachers, gurus, preachers, speakers, and coaches.

Uttara Phalguni is less comfort-oriented nakshatra. This is actually the place where you rip the fruit from the fig tree. Uttara gives tremendous opportunities for growth and creative expansion. The animal of this nakshatra is the bull, which is strong, hard-working, target-oriented, and dangerous. We associate the animal with Nandi – the bull that Shiva rides, which is famous for its devotion and loyalty. That's why Uttara Phalguni natives are very loyal. It is said that when Shiva drank the poison from the ocean of milk, some of it fell on the ground and Nandi drank it and helped saving the world.

Deity

The ruling deity of Uttara Phalguni is **Aryaman**- the God of patronage and friendship. Aryaman is one of the Adityas, the solar deities. He is also called the God of Sacred laws, contracts and unions and has a special connection with the matrimonial union. It is said that the best nakshatra for marriage is Uttara Phalguni. Purva is more towards the romantic part before the marriage, while Uttara is the actual marriage and commitment. Aryaman is the divine matchmaker. Uttara makes the marriage beautiful and harmonious.

Uttara Phalguni and Aryaman are associated with friendship, helping other people, and receiving help. Uttara is generous and eager to help the one in need. Aryaman is the god of kindness and favors, too, which makes the native of this nakshatra kind and cultured.

Aryaman is famous for his leadership qualities, for his honor, nobility, and connection with traditions and ancestors.

Uttara Phalguni also has a connection to Lord Ganesha and the warrior Arjuna. Ganesh Chaturthi, which is a Hindu festival celebrating the birth of the God Ganesha, usually happens when Sun is in Uttara Phalguni.

Key Points

1. Uttara Phalguni people can be very sexual. Natives with malefic influence can work in the field of the sex industry.

2. Uttara Phalguni natives can be great leaders. This nakshatra puts you on a stage, on a platform where people will watch you or listen to you like a guru. These natives are very ambitious, hard-working, target-oriented and dangerous like a bull in the professional field. They want to achieve great success.

3. Uttara people are extremely creative and artistic. They are cultured, kind, friendly, attractive, and sexy.

4. Uttara natives are good at making contracts and agreements. They can be great astrologers, lawyers, counsellors, speakers, HR specialists, and critics. They are very good at communication and writing.

5. Uttara Phalguni natives may be interested in music, dance, or yoga. The reason is that Nandi provided the music when Shiva performed his tandava dance (Nataraja).

6. Uttara Phalguni natives can be extremely fortunate in life – they will receive opportunities for great achievements, success, and fame. This nakshatra gives enjoyment and pleasure.

7. Marriage and commitment are important for these natives. They are one of the most loyal

friends and spouses. This nakshatra symbolizes the union of two people and the vows and promises they give to each other. Love and commitment matter!!! Of course, if there is malefic influence in your chart, associated with this nakshatra, the result will be the opposite.

8. These people are generous, they want to help and change society. They use their success and authority for the betterment of the world. Healing the suffering of people plays a crucial role for these natives.

9. Uttara Phalguni natives are closely connected with Ganesha- that's why they are brilliant writers, love traveling as Ganesha does on his giant rat to faraway places, and they can be excellent at doing business.

10. These people may have some kind of obsessive-compulsive disorder.

11. They may love watching documentary movies.

12. Uttara's natives have special karma with weddings – there can be some unusual event that happened on their wedding, or they had a strange/different wedding ceremony. My Vedic teachers always said that these people have a divine match – they will get a karmic partner! Once they get married, their life will change.

13. It is said that these natives will have more difficult life and challenges till the age of 32 years. Then their life will start to improve gradually and the culmination of their success and prosperity will be after the age of 38 years towards their 50s.

14. They could benefit from the patronage of others.

15. If malefic planets are aspecting this nakshatra it can lead to troubles and scandals.

16. It is said that Uttara Phalguni natives may not get their father's inheritance, or they may have to fight to get it. This is because, in mythology, Ganesha rejected his father's wealth.

17. These people may have major connections with bulls- they may be a fan of a sports team, which has a bull as a symbol, like the Chicago Bulls, or would love visiting places or restaurants, associated with bulls or similar animals.

Remedies

The best remedy for this nakshatra is to have beautiful furniture and especially beds. If you have a broken bed or couch in your home, you should fix them immediately.

You can buy a Ganesha statue or an elephant statue with beautiful tusks and a trunk. Another remedy is to take a statue of a strong bull.

Careers/Hobbies

Uttara Phalguni nakshatra may produce professions (or hobbies) related to:

- Art and creativity, media and communication

- The entertainment industry, show business and everything related to celebrities.

- Sex and sex appeal

- Gurus, teachers, preachers; advisers, counsellors

- All professions that put you on a stage – motivational speakers, influencers, etc.

- Matchmaking, weddings, and marriages

- Professions associated with authority, power, and leadership – CEOs, managers, etc.

- Politics, government, laws, and contracts

- Healing and medicine

- Charity, donations, philanthropy

Examples

Famous people with prominent Uttara Phalguni nakshatra are Harrison Ford, Tiger Woods, and Sophia Loren. For example, Sophia Loren has her Sun in the tenth house in Uttara Phalguni, which bestows her success and worldly fame. She is one of the sex symbols of the 20th century, she is talented and although she had a difficult childhood, she managed to reach the heights of cinema and won an Oscar award for her role in the movie "Two Women". Sophia Loren is a real benefic manifestation of Uttara Phalguni nakshatra – Sun is in its own constellation, in his favorite house, where it has Dig Bala (directional strength) – definitely she was born to be seen and recognized!

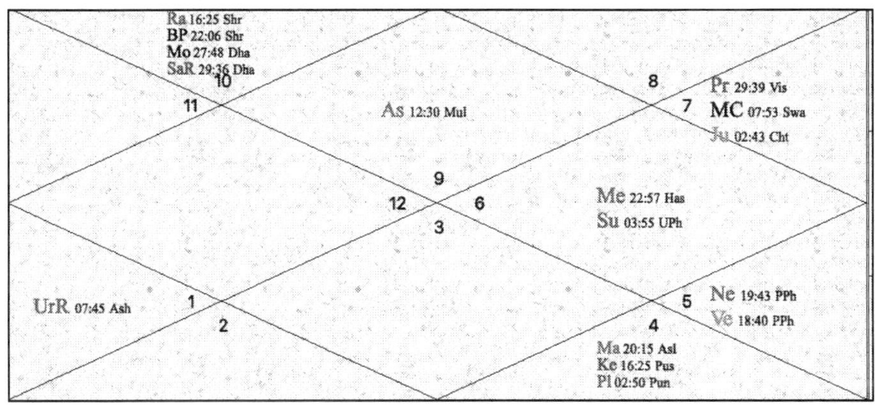

HASTA

The Hand

ZODIAC RANGE	10°00' VIRGO - 23°20' VIRGO
RULING PLANET	MOON
DEITY	SAVITAR
SYMBOL	PALM OF A HAND
CASTE	MERCHANT
ANIMAL	FEMALE BUFFALO
SOUNDS	PU, SHAA, NA, THA
MAIN FIXED STARS	MU VIRGINIS, ALGORAB, GIENAH
PADAS	PADA 1- ARIES PADA 2- TAURUS PADA 3- GEMINI PADA 4- CANCER
COLOR	DARK GREEN
GENDER	MALE NAKSHATRA
KEY WORDS	INTELLIGENT, SKILLFUL, HUMOUROUS,

Meaning

Hasta is the thirteenth nakshatra in the zodiac belt. It lies entirely in the zodiac sign Virgo. Hasta is a mix of the energy not only of Virgo, its ruler Mercury and the nakshatra's ruler Moon but the Sun, too (because of the ruling God). The Mercurial energy, combined with the Moon energy makes these natives very intelligent. As you know the Moon and Mercury rule the mind in Vedic Astrology and this constellation may give a brilliant mind and intellect. However, the Moon's influence here makes the people more sensitive, moody and insecure.

Hasta means "the hand" and the symbol of the nakshatra is a palm of a hand or a fist. An alternative translation of the name of this constellation is "laughter"- "Has" means to laugh. This indicates that Hasta natives are funny and pleasant. The palm of a hand symbolizes not only skillfulness and effort but knowledge, destiny and fate. The hand is associated with working and putting effort into something. The other symbol – the fist- is associated with ambition and determination on the positive side, but on the negative side, it indicates anger, greed, inability to let go of things, and manipulation.

The animal associated with this constellation is the female buffalo, which indicates strength, patience and hard-working. Buffaloes love water, so Hasta natives want to live next to water. We relate the animal with the myth of Mahisha, which means buffalo, and Durga. Buffalo is also known as the ride of Lord Yama. So, Mahisha was a demon, who conquered the world of Gods. Then the Gods decided to create Durga and gave her their powers. Durga was able to kill the demon Mahisha and turn back the kingdom to the Gods. This is the reason why Hasta natives should be careful with their negative traits – they have to kill their inner demon Mahisha. Hasta can be an open palm, symbolizing blessing and destiny, but it can be an angry fist, which can hurt people.

In one of the astrology courses that I had previously enrolled in, the teacher mentioned that Hasta nakshatra is a "widow maker" nakshatra, but he didn't explain why....Of course, I am a Virgo and started my own investigation of why this nakshatra can make you lose your spouse untimely and Voila...I found it out! In the portion of Hasta nakshatra, you can find a fixed star, called Vindemiatrix – it is around 15° Virgo. This is a malefic star that gives disgrace and often causes the natives to become widows/widowers. Of course, I have it prominent in my chart...I am so lucky, right? However, now I understand why I always have this feeling in me that my partner will die before me....I am single, still, I have this thought in my mind very often. Nakshatras really explain your life in a unique way.

Hasta nakshatra is the place, where Mercury is exalted, so all traits of Mercury can be seen in the Hasta natives.

Deity

The ruling deity of Hasta is **Savitar**, the Sun God. Savitar is one of the Adityas, he is a form of Surya. Savitar is the god, who imparts creative and transforming energy. "Savita" means awakener, rouser. This God inspires and awakes us. Savitar is connected to the sunrise. Savitar brings light and creation. He is the god, who gives life, like the Sun gives life to this planet. He is the reason why Hasta nakshatra is associated with creation, creative energy and childbirth. Savitar not only brings light, but he brings vision to people – enabling your eyes to see the world. Sun God is a vivifier and makes Hasta natives inspirational and visionary people.

Savitar is jovial, pleasant, and funny, he likes tricks and games.

Savitar is supposed to be extremely skilled with his hands. Sun God is illustrated with golden hands, which figuratively means that everything he touches turns to gold. Savitar will give Hasta natives everything they want in their hands. Of course, if there is a malefic influence, the natives can become fraudsters, robbers, gamblers, and tricksters.

Hasta is one of the most positive, creative and optimistic nakshatra.

Savitar is said to be the God of the Divine Weapons, too, which makes the natives great warriors in life and always ready for battle.

Savitar is invoked in the famous Gayatri Mantra, which is very esoteric and is supposed to contain the deepest secrets of the Universe. Savitar is known to guard the world of spirits and the occult. He is known to increase the life of humans and Gods. In Rig Veda, Savitar is the one who brings all two-footed and four-footed beings to home or rest (death) and awakens them, giving them life.

Key Points

1. Hasta natives are very pleasant, lighthearted, positive, creative, funny, and charming. They may love games, magic tricks, jokes, gambling, playing cards and sports.

2. Hasta natives are intelligent and hard-working. They are very skillful, especially with their hands. Hasta is associated with everything that is done with hands. Whatever they touch turns into gold.

3. This nakshatra can bring a lot of money. Hasta people can bring back to life like Savitar – if you

have a company or project that goes in a bad direction, Hasta natives can bring it back to life and make it successful. These people can be prosperous in all industries. Extremely flexible and adaptable individuals.

4. Hasta natives have the good and bad qualities of the planet Mercury – good at writing, speaking, sales, public relations, communication, good at multitasking, good at skills and talents connected to hands like painting, sculpting, crafting, sowing, etc.

5. Hasta natives can be extremely influential and visionary individuals. They can be like the Sun, bringing light to people, and helping others to heal, make them smile and laugh.

6. Hasta natives are good at occult fields like astrology, reiki, palmistry, and mantras.

7. It is said that these people will build stable and successful life between the age of 30 and 42 and would receive great affluence if they live beyond 64 years.

8. They could have dark secrets of sexual intimacy and sometimes incest.

9. A distant relative or a stranger can leave them a large fortune or inheritance.

10. Hasta nakshatra is a fast nakshatra – natives like doing things in a fast manner. Together with Ashwini and Swati, it gives results very quickly. If you want to have immediate results in something, do it when Moon transits in these nakshatras.

11. Hasta natives love water and love taking long showers. They may love dealing with gold and cash, too. Hasta people may love shaking

hands. These natives are connected to the earth and the plants, so very often they become vegetarians or when they want to lose weight, they try only plant-based meals.

12.   Hasta natives have a great sense of humor and often write in their chats phrases like "ha ha ha"

13.   These people are very active and always have to do something- whether it's fixing something, writing, or if there is nothing to do, then they'll be on their phones.

14.   Hasta natives can lose their spouses untimely. If there is malefic influence, the natives can be arrogant, manipulative, deceptive, cunning, critical, and even they can become fraudsters and criminals.

Remedies

The best remedy for this nakshatra natives is to go regularly for a massage of the hands and pay attention to the way their hands look – they should always be beautiful and healthy.

Another remedy is to do activities with your hands – play sports, paint, fix something in your house, etc. You can listen to Gayatri Mantra or watch comedy movies and shows.

Careers/Hobbies

Hasta nakshatra may produce professions (or hobbies) related to:

- Professions in all types of industries, where you use your hands constantly, manual labor

- Healing and childbirth – doctors, nurses, midwives,

- Humor, entertainment and comedy

- Astrology, occult, palmistry

- All artistic and creative professions associated with hands – writers, sculptors, painters, etc.

- Sales, communication, and public relations

- Professions associated with the travel and hospitality industry, plants, and the earth.

Examples

I will give you an example of one of my clients, who booked a career consultation with me. She has Mercury and Venus in Hasta. Mercury is exalted; still, Hasta is not the best place for Venus – it is debilitated here. However, we see the Neechabhanga yoga, which cancels the debilitation. The interesting part is that Mercury is the ruler of the 5th house – the house of children and it is placed in Hasta. My client works as a midwife and helps women to give birth. The other interesting thing is that she has enrolled in many reiki and astrology courses and like the occult side of the world.

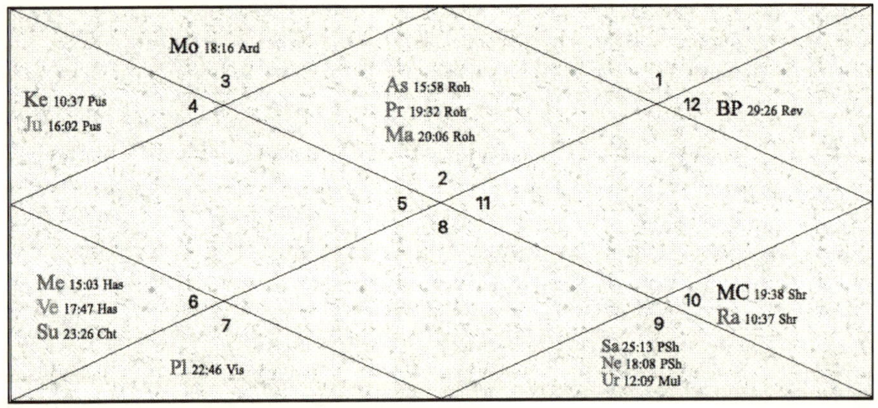

CHITRA

The Star of opportunity

ZODIAC RANGE	23°20' VIRGO - 6°40' LIBRA
RULING PLANET	MARS
DEITY	TVASHTAR
SYMBOL	PEARL
CASTE	FARMER
ANIMAL	FEMALE TIGER
SOUNDS	PAY, PO, RAA, REE
MAIN FIXED STARS	SPICA
PADAS	PADA 1- LEO PADA 2- VIRGO PADA 3- LIBRA PADA 4- SCORPIO
COLOR	BLACK
GENDER	FEMALE NAKSHATRA
KEY WORDS	CHARMING, ARTISTIC, SHINING

Meaning

Chitra is the fourteenth nakshatra in the zodiac belt. It overlaps two zodiac signs – starts at 23°20' Virgo and ends at 6°40' Libra. On the first part, Chitra is a mix of the energy of Virgo, Mercury, and Mars, which is the ruler of this nakshatra. On the second side, Chitra is influenced by the traits of the Libra, Venus, and Mars again. Mars gives this nakshatra a lot of energy, mechanical skills, and intelligence. On Virgo's side Chitra is more detailed oriented, materialistic, skillful, and technical, while on Libra's side, it is more focused on harmony, beauty, fashion, and sensual artistic side of the world due to the combination of the Martian and Venusian energy.

What is Libra? Libra is artistic and beautiful. It rules love, romance, marriages, harmony, markets and courts, other people, and the masses.

Chitra means "beautiful", "shining", "glittering" or "many colors", which shows us that Chitra natives will be shining and beautiful or will like glittering, colorful clothes, and objects. The symbol of the constellation is a pearl or a gem. The pearl symbolizes the True Self of the individual that is hiding behind hard shells. You can find the pearls in the oyster shells, but we need to break the shell in order to take them...it's the same with our inner self – we need to change and transform in order to find who we really are. So, finding yourself is a difficult process. The animal of the nakshatra is a female tiger. These animals are very beautiful, gracious, with a specific character, and extremely dangerous.

The Chitra animal is connected to the myth of Ayyappa and the milk of the tigress. Ayyappa was a child of Shiva and Mohini (female form of Vishnu). He incarnated as Manikantan. He was alone in the jungle when the queen Raja Rajasekhara found him and adopted him. The queen never wanted someone else's child to take on the kingdom and tried to secretly kill him by giving him a task she knew he would fail and die – she requested a milk from a tigress. Manikantan not only came back from his mission alive, but he came riding the tigress, followed by her cubs.

Chitra is the nakshatra, where you can find one of the most auspicious fixed stars- Spica. It is placed around 29° Virgo. Spica or Alpha Virginis gives success, wealth, and fame- it literally can make you a star, a celebrity.

Deity

The ruling deity of Chitra is **Tvashtar** (also known as Vishvakarma). Tvashtar is the creator of the universe, the Celestial Architect. He can create new forms from the ones that already exist, so he is something like a celestial designer. This is the reason that Chitra natives are extremely talented in the field of design, architecture, art, and fashion, jewelry.

Tvashtar is the one who created the different lokas – the kingdom of the Gods, humans, the kingdom of the demons, the underworld of the Nagas. Some Vedic scholars explained Tvashtar as an abstract deity, something like Aditi, who is the space. Tvastar's creative energy is before existing of Brahma and Brahma used that energy to create the Universe. It is said that the physical form of Tvastar is Vishvakarma.

Tvashtar created the illusion, Maya, which sustains this world. He is the one who created all buildings, parks, and statues in the different kingdoms, he is the one who created the divine weapons for the Gods, such as Vajra for Indra, a chalice for Soma, Sudarshana Chakra for Vishnu, Trishula for Shiva. The creation of spaceships and flying cities are associated with this deity, too. Tvashtar is the father of Viswarupa or Trishira (the 3 headed demon), who was killed by Indra, and in revenge, Tvashtar created Vritra, the great dragon. Tvashtar had many daughters and one of them is Sanjana, who is the wife of Surya.

Chitra is also connected with Chitragupta - celestial accountant. He is the one who keeps accounts and records of all souls.

Key Points

1. Chitra natives are one of the most skillful and technically gifted individuals – they can be extremely good at design, architecture, art, fashion, and any fields that require technical or mechanical skills and knowledge. They are good at keeping records and accounting, programming, and creating algorithms.

2. Chitra is one of the nakshatras, which really embodies the creation process. These natives need to create and put their talents into something.

3. All Mars-ruled nakshatras have a dual nature – they are always situated between 2 zodiac signs - Mrigashira – between Taurus and Gemini, Chitra between Virgo and Libra, and Dhanishta – between Capricorn and Aquarius. So, this duality will influence the natives of these nakshatras.

4. Chitra natives are associated with the Maya, the illusion that sustains our world. This can be seen in their life as a love for magic, illusions, tricks, or creating some kind of illusion, or even it can be associated with artificial intellect and virtual reality, 3D reality.

5. Chitra natives love structures, frames, constructions, forms, and levels. They love vision boards and board games, too.

6. Chitra natives are interested in weapons, spaceships, and jewels. It is said that if Chitra natives receive a jewel as a present, it will bring them luck and opportunities.

7. Chitra natives are very beautiful and charismatic. They like to shine and attract attention. They can be stylish, too. They usually wear bright and colorful clothing and jewelry. Chitra natives have a fondness for flowers, garlands, and other objects of natural beauty.

8. Chitra people can be famous.

9. Chitra people love photos and movies and very often they can work as photographers or in the movie industry. They love manipulating pictures with different effects. They may have a photographic memory. Basically, these people are perceiving and understanding the world, through their eyes and vision. So, they want to see the things in order to understand them.

10. Due to the mythology of Tvashtar, Chitra people may have many children (around 3). This nakshatra can produce mainly daughters and one of them may get married to a very powerful person.

11. Chitra people are excellent in astrology and occult fields. Chitra can give us the fruit of our good karma. It has strong spiritual energy and effect.

12. Chitra people may wake up often between 3 am and 4 am, or they may stay awake till that time. This is due to the animal of the constellation – the female tiger. If Chitra is your Ascendant, you may have very beautiful face and eyes.

13.   Chitra natives may have strong sexual desires as a part of their creative energy. They can be jealous of the people, who want to outshine them. They may have a lot of enemies, who will bring obstructions in their career growth. They may have serious disputes with their father and senior colleagues, or bosses. This is due to the myth that Tvashtar had a bad relationship with Indra.

14.   Chitra natives may live away from their homeland.

15.   Chitra people pay attention to the way they look – they like modeling and sculpting their bodies and you can see them in the fitness and bodybuilding industry.

16.   These natives may love doing things at the last moment

17.   Chitra natives are very social and have many friends.

18.   Chitra natives have a strong theme with stepmothers and losing from their sibling. This comes from the myth of Ayyappa.

19.   Chitra natives should never be challenged as they will always win.

20.   Chitra people may like collecting exclusive things.

Remedies

The best remedy for this nakshatra is to put in order all photos that you have – delete the one you don't need or cause your pain and trouble. You can put photos of your family around your house, too.

The other good remedy is to have a statue of beautiful tiger.

If you want your dreams to come true, you can try to use a vision board. As I mentioned, Chitra natives perceive the world through their eyes.

If you receive a jewelry as a present, it is good to wear it, because it can bring you luck.

Careers/Hobbies

Chitra nakshatra may produce professions (or hobbies) related to:

-   Craftsman, architecture, design

-   Photography and movie making

-   Fashion, beauty industry, jewelry, modeling

-   Professions associated with illusions and different realities

-   Professions associated with creative energy – artists, musicians, painters.

-   Professions associated with technical and mechanical skills, and production of machinery- mechanics, computer programmers, etc.

-   Occult and magic

Examples

I will give you again an example of one of my clients, who booked a yearly horoscope reading with me. This person has Ascendant and Sun in Chitra from the Virgo's side and Saturn in Chitra, from the Libra's sign. So, this constellation plays a crucial role in his natal chart.

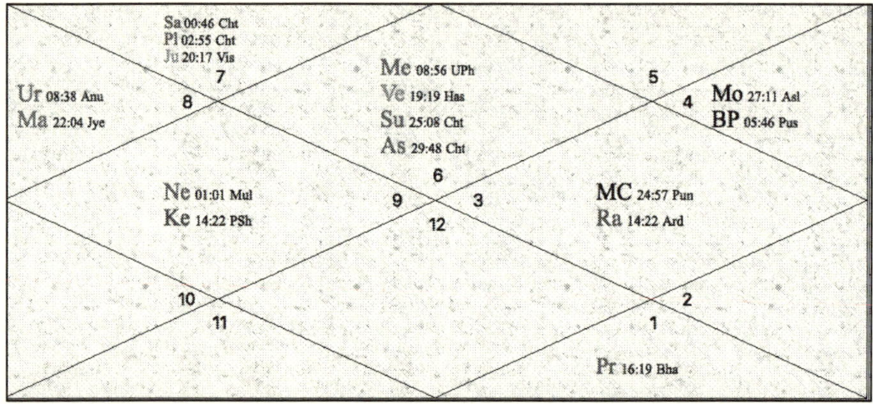

The first manifestation of Chitra is that this individual is an architect, and he is interested in creating different small jewels as additional source of income – like earrings and bracelets. The other Chitra manifestation is that he had a stepmother- the good news is that he was in good relationship with her, and she did not want to kill him like Manikantan. The other interesting thing is when he was young, he wanted to become magician and make magic tricks, which is associated with Maya and illusion.

SWATI

The Self-Going Star

ZODIAC RANGE	6°40' LIBRA - 20°00' LIBRA
RULING PLANET	RAHU
DEITY	VAYU
SYMBOL	FRESH PLANT IN THE WIND
CASTE	BUTCHER
ANIMAL	MALE BUFFALO
SOUNDS	RU, RAY, RA, TA
MAIN FIXED STARS	ARCTURUS
PADAS	PADA 1- SAGITTARIUS PADA 2- CAPRICORN PADA 3- AQUARIUS PADA 4- PISCES
COLOR	BLACK
GENDER	FEMALE NAKSHATRA
KEY WORDS	INDIPENDENT, RESTLESS, EAGER TO LEARN, FRAGILE

Meaning

Swati is the fifteenth nakshatra in the zodiac belt. It lies entirely in the zodiac sign Libra. Swati is influenced by the traits of the Libra, Venus, and the ruler of this constellation- Rahu. As I mentioned before, all nakshatras that are ruled by Rahu are eccentric, futuristic, and out of the box. Rahu is the head without a body, which always wants to eat and get all the material blessings! You also know that Venus rules the trade and the markets, and masses, so the combination of Rahu, Libra, and Venus can create great businessmen and great professionals. Swati natives can be full of business and entrepreneurial ideas. Sun is debilitated in Swati and these people should be careful not to misuse their powers and learn how to cooperate with others.

Swati means "independent", "self-going", or a sword, which tells us that Swati natives love their freedom and are ready for a battle. Individuality is a key word for this constellation. The symbol of Swati is grass, blown by the wind or a coral. The first symbol is associated with movement, restlessness, and freedom. Wind can be very powerful, still, it can be gentle and pleasant. The grass is associated with freshness. The other symbol – the coral- is related to beauty and its ability to propagate by itself and impact the environment it lives. This is why Swati people have an influence on the world around them and society. The animal of this nakshatra is male buffalo. It is strong, patient, and hard-working. Buffalo is related to Yama and his brother Shani (Saturn). Shani is exalted in Swati, so these natives will have some of the good traits of Saturn like strength and willpower.

Deity

The ruling deity of Swati is **Vayu**, the God of the Wind and Celestial musicians. Vayu is connected with the prana and oxygen. Vayu is a life-giving breath that nourishes the beings on the planet.

Vayu is the father of one of the greatest warriors in Hindu mythology – Hanuman and Bhima. All qualities of Vayu are manifested in Hanuman – intelligence, wisdom, loyalty, and letting off the Ego. When Hanuman was young, he thought that the Sun was a big fruit and jumped into the sky to eat it. The Sun God felt irritated by the little child and asked Indra to bring the child down with his weapon. Hanuman was struck on his jaw by Indra's weapon, the thunderbolt. Impressed by the child's resistance, the Gods blessed Hanuman with various powers, but he started making jokes with others and the Gods cursed him to forget his gifts. When he apologized for his mistake, Gods said his powers would come back when someone remind him about them. Later on, he gained his powers back and become one of the most loyal and brave warriors. Hanuman is associated with the myths of Lord Rama, Sita, Jambavan, and Vibhishana.

In Swati, you can find a constant theme associated with ego, individuality, and competitiveness. There is a story about one big beautiful tree that no storm could ever blow away his fruits and leaves. The tree became very proud and "Ego-centric" and thought that it is stronger than the God Vayu. When the Wind King heard that, he came to the tree and blew away all the leaves and fruits that the tree had and said to the tree, that many years ago Brahma rested in the shades of that tree and Vayu paid respect to this place, because he considered it as sacred. So it's not his power that made it great, but Vayu's grace. This story tells us that we should be careful with our Ego and we should always know that our powers are granted by God and the universe.

Swati is associated with another deity, too – Saraswati, the Goddess of music and learning.

Key Points

1. Swati natives are full of ideas – one of the best entrepreneurs and businesspeople can be seen with prominent Swati nakshatra. These natives have influence in society.

2. Swati natives are like the wind – independent, free, both gentle and destructive. The wind is fast, and it is moving all the time. It spreads all over the world. This is the reason why Swati people are free and with strong individuality. They want to travel and experience the world; they may be obsessed with knowing what is happening in the world in general.

3. Air is associated with communication, so Swati people are extremely good at communication and spreading information – good at marketing, PR, media, and all fields associated with information and data. If you want something to be heard and known, you should find a Swati person for this task. Especially if you have a marketing agency, I think you should hire mainly Swati natives.

4. All Rahu-ruled nakshatras are interested in the cosmos, rockets, and airplanes.

5. Swati people love music and love playing different musical instruments. They love the wind and watching tornados. Swati people love flying objects and flying superheroes like Superman. They also love water, due to the animal of this constellation.

6. Swati people should know how to breathe correctly! Breathing is extremely important for them. It is good for their bodies and mind to go to aerobics, yoga, and different breathing

practices. Vayu is the prana – the energy that gives life!

7. Swati nakshatra people will need a mentor or a coach, who can "remind them of their powers and gifts" like the story of Hanuman.

8. Swati people have big goals and give everything to fulfill them – this is again associated with the myth of Hanuman, who wanted to eat the Sun. They want to reach the top and they have no fear.

9. Swati people have a lot of common traits with the Chitra people. This is because the yogatara of Swati is 0° of Libra. Yogatara is the brightest star of one nakshatra and it is considered the most powerful place from the constellation.

10.   Swati people may become vegetarians. They take care of the way they look and want to have nice and beautifully sculptured bodies. They should be careful with their jaws.

11.   Swati natives may live abroad, especially if this nakshatra is associated with third, ninth, and twelfth houses in their natal chart

12.   Swati natives are restless. They cannot stick to one particular thought. They should pay attention to their ego and individuality. If there is a malefic influence, their ego will become their greatest weakness. These natives may be indecisive and the type of people, who cannot stand up for themselves.

13.   If there are afflicted planets in Swati, especially in the second house of the horoscope, natives may have bad breath or harsh speech.

14. Swati people have all the qualities of Hanuman – kind, loyal, brave, great diplomats, and adventurous.

15. Swati people may have ADHD (attention-deficit hyperactivity disorder) or OCD (obsessive-compulsive disorder).

16. Swati people may love shoes or there can be something specific related to shoes in their life. These natives may have a specific way of walking, too. This comes again from the yogatara of the nakshatra, which is near the leg of the maiden from Virgo zodiac sign.

Remedies

The best remedy for this nakshatra is to have beautiful shoes – they should always be clean and neat.

In one of the astrology courses, the teacher taught us that when Swati natives buy new shoes, new love is coming into their life, or they meet a new person for dating. Of course, this depends on so many factors. Just for the experiment, you can buy shoes with the color of the planet that is placed in Swati and see what will happen. I tried this technique in my personal life, but unfortunately, nobody appeared. However, my natal chart is a little bit more specific, so it will be interesting for me whether this technique works for you and let see if you will meet someone.

Other remedies are to master breathing yoga techniques or play a musical instrument.

Careers/Hobbies

Swati nakshatra may produce professions (or hobbies) related to:

- Communication and information

- Businessmen and entrepreneurs of all types

- Music and singing

- The travel industry, aerospace, and airplanes

- Fashion industry – especially dealing with shoes

- Markets and trading

- Politicians and diplomats

- Sports, yoga, meditation, and breathing

- All professions that are associated with air and wind.

Examples

The most famous representatives of Swati nakshatra are Charlie Chaplin, Mahatma Gandhi, Bill Gates, and Hilary Clinton.

The interesting part here is that one of the most iconic scenes in the history of cinema is "The `bread roll ballet' from 1925's movie - `The Gold Rush'". In this scene, Charlie Chaplin takes 2 bread rolls, put them on forks <u>as shoes</u>, and starts simulating a dance on the dinner table. Furthermore, you can see that shoes play an important role in his movies – in one of them, he even boils and eats his shoe! The other interesting trait of Chaplin is the way he walks in his movies. So, these are some of the manifestations of Swati in the life of Charlie Chaplin.

VISHAKHA

The Star of Purpose

ZODIAC RANGE	20°00' LIBRA - 3°20' SCORPIO
RULING PLANET	JUPITER
DEITY	INDRA, AGNI
SYMBOL	ARCHWAY
CASTE	OUTCASTE
ANIMAL	MALE TIGER
SOUNDS	TE, TU, TAY, TO
MAIN FIXED STARS	ALPHA LIBRAE, BETA LIBRAE, GAMMA LIBRAE, IOTA LIBRAE
PADAS	PADA 1- ARIES PADA 2- TAURUS PADA 3- GEMINI PADA 4- CANCER
COLOR	GOLDEN
GENDER	FEMALE NAKSHATRA
KEY WORDS	COURAGE, AMBITIOUS, GOALS, CONQUEST OF ENEMIES

Meaning

Vishakha is the sixteenth nakshatra in the zodiac belt. It overlaps two zodiac signs – Vishakha starts at 20°00' Libra and ends at 3°20' Scorpio. So, in the first part, this constellation is a mixture of the energies of Libra, Venus, and Jupiter, which is the ruler of Vishakha. In the second part... the situation gets darker – you will feel the deep energy of Scorpio, Mars and Ketu, which are both the rulers of this zodiac sign, and again Jupiter.

What is Scorpio? As I have written in my book "Vedic Astrology – Easy&Simple", Scorpio is the most karmic zodiac sign in Vedic Astrology and brings karmic events in the house, it is placed. Scorpio is deep, intense, secretive, mystical, obsessive, and scandalous. Scorpio rules death and rebirth, transformation, hidden world, occult, psychology, sex, and research.

So, Vishakha nakshatra has a totally different energy. Libra's part is dealing more with the material world, while the Scorpio part goes deep into the "swamp" and the natives start searching for a change and transformation. Jupiter will bring knowledge and wisdom, and expansion of horizons. Moon and Rahu are debilitated in Scorpio.

Vishakha means "the forked one" or "two branches". An alternative name is Radha, which means "the delightful one". Vishakha is associated with goals, purpose, and reaching success. That is why it is called "the star of purpose". The symbol of the nakshatra is an archway or gateway or potter wheel. The archway has multiple meanings- some associate it with victory and welcoming back the warriors after victory, and others connect it with spiritual development – passing from the material world to the spiritually oriented world. The other symbol – the gateway- is often depicted with leaves, and it is associated with different ceremonies like marriage ceremonies. It is again a symbol of triumph. The potter wheel is associated with life and shaping that life as a part of our destiny.

Definitely, Vishakha is a nakshatra that is striving for triumph! It is ready to do everything to reach the goal. These natives can get very obsessive about their plans and decisions. As I previously said, all Jupiter-ruled nakshatras are heavy, so Vishakha natives should be careful with their desire to win over the enemies, because sometimes, especially in the Scorpio part, your biggest enemy is you, yourself.

The animal of the constellation is a male tiger – again dangerous, proud, independent, and strong animal, which traits somehow describe the Vishakha natives.

Deity

Vishakha is the only nakshatra that has two deities- **Indra**, the King of Gods and God of Wars and Rain, and **Agni**, the God of fire. Some astrologers consider that there is some misunderstanding of Rig Veda and Mahabharata, and that the ruling deity are not Indra and Agni, but another deity called **Indragni**. However, we will keep to the version of two deities- the one that is taught in the Hindu astrology courses.

Indra is the chief among the Gods – he is a great warrior and loves enjoying life – he lives in a beautiful palace full of luxury and pleasures, drinking Soma, and having beautiful women around him. Indra is the one who slays a lot of demons. He killed the demons Visvarupa and Vitra, who stole all the water on the planet and in this way, Indra brought the water back to the earth.

Indra is famous for his desire for pleasure. He had an affair with the wife of Rishi Gautama – Ahilya. Indra was obsessed with Ahilya and transformed himself into her husband and made love with her. When Rishi Gautama saw them, he cursed Indra to have his body covered with 1000 yonis (vaginas). Ashamed, Indra went into isolation, and when other Gods found out about this, they begged Brahma to help Indra. Brahma went to sage Gautama and the thousand yonis turned into thousand eyes.

Indra is the king of Gods; however, he can be insecure and deceptive, too. He can have a big ego with which he hides his insecurities. Indra represents the desires, impulsive nature, and insecurity of the human mind. He did not want to let go of his power and throne. So, to protect his position as the king, he kept disturbing the penance of others.

The other deity Agni is the God of fire and is associated mainly with Krittika nakshatra. Agni's creative fire manifests into power and courage toward the desires of the natives. Fire, especially if the natives are obsessed with their desires, can have negative effects and cause harm.

As you can see, Vishakha nakshatra has an extreme duality – not only it has 2 deities, but the name of the constellation means two branches. This tells us that the natives will have dual nature, too – two personalities and swings in mood.

Key Points

1. Vishakha nakshatra is chaotic nakshatra – there can be a lot of ups and downs in the life of natives.

2. Vishakha people are goal-oriented, and they have a purpose in life. They are ambitious and competitive. They want success at any cost and are ready to do everything in order to win the battle. They always want to be the champion

and drink the Soma. They can be seen as megalomaniacs and egocentrics.

3. Vishakha natives have dual nature and personalities, and there is a theme in their life of splitting something into two parts or branches. If there are malefic influences, these people may become bipolar, have big mood swings or even they can have schizophrenia.

4. Vishakha natives love luxurious life – they want to have beautiful homes and enjoy the pleasures of life. They want a lavish lifestyle – having the best cars, flying first class, etc. Often in their homes, you will see something like an arch or gateway. Whenever Vishakha natives enter a home or a workplace with an arch or pillars, they may achieve success. This symbol brings them luck.

5. Vishakha natives will have a lot of insecurities. This will be the reason why they will strive for success – they need to feel secure somehow.

6. Decisions play an important role here. Vishakha natives are always making decisions and very often they totally change their decisions. They may start doing something and, in a few minutes, change their mind and start doing something else. There can be confusion and frustration. They always have a third opinion.

7. These natives have a karmic relationship with their father. They may seduce another person's spouse.

8. Vishakha natives love the occult, they may love milk products and colors. Vishakha natives can be very good friends with Ashlesha natives.

9. Vishakha natives may have a big transformation in their career at age 34.

Whatever they create in their life, will be long-lasting, withstanding the test of time.

10. Vishakha natives may have an association with ceremonies, especially marriage ceremonies. This is due to the gateway symbol of this constellation.

11. Vishakha people can be very obsessive and jealous. The nature of this nakshatra can be summarized in two words - "Fixation" and "Obsession". Vishakha natives cannot take defeat by another person.

12. Vishakha natives are intense and passionate. They are generally candid, speak the truth, and always believe in their core values. Three padas of Vishakha falls in Libra and the native usually find their balance between the material and the spiritual world. The fourth pada however falls in Scorpio and the planets in this zone go through a lot of metamorphosis.

13. Vishakha people may have the same tiger traits as Chitra natives – they may stay awake till 3 am/4 am or always wake up around that time. They can have beautiful eyes and strong eyesight.

14. The potter's wheel shows the creative and artistic side of Vishakha natives, especially on the Libra's side.

15. Vishakha natives can be extremely sexual! They can be obsessed with porn, masturbation, and they can be lustful for every beautiful female or male. This comes from the myth of Indra and the 1000 vaginas.

16. The myth, related to the thousand eyes of Indra can make the Vishakha natives obsessed

of spying on others and can create an interest in secret societies like the Masons and Illuminati.

Remedies

The best remedy for this nakshatra is to have an arch in your home or a picture/ statue of an arch. The other remedy is to have a statue of a tiger. You should have beautiful cutlery set, especially forks ! If you have a broken fork, throw it away or buy another set.

It is beneficial to have your own spiritual rituals, especially involving fire – you can meditate and lit candles in the room for example.

Careers/Hobbies

Vishakha nakshatra may produce professions (or hobbies) related to:

- Military, police, detectives, and guards

- Professions associated with researching

- Professions associated with pleasures and leisure time – this is due to Indra and his love for pleasures like drinking, dancing, and gambling.

- Sex and lustful life

- Politics, business, and finance

- Professions associated with fire – cooks, bakers, etc.

- Occult and spirituality

Examples

I will give you again example with one of my clients.

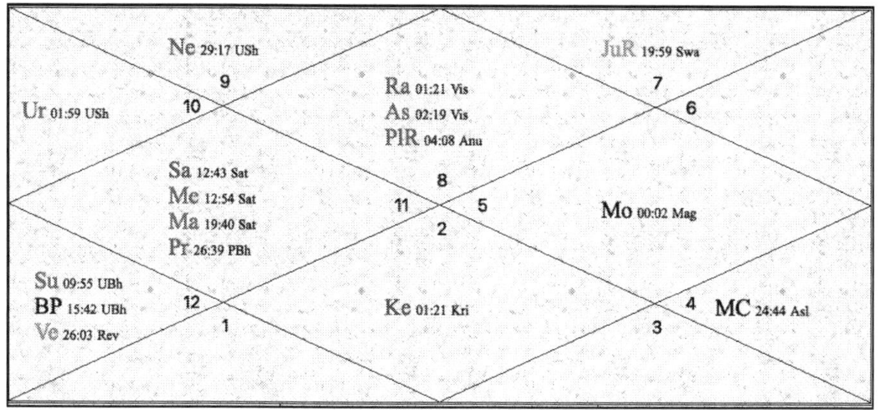

So, this is a person, who has an Ascendant and Rahu in the Scorpio part of Vishakha. Basically, Rahu is debilitated in Scorpio, and this makes the whole situation very difficult. This client was a very obsessed person and could not find mental peace. He booked with me a career consultation because he wanted so much to succeed in his business venture, that he could not think of anything else. He wanted to be the King...like Indra, but unfortunately, when Ego and insecurities are controlling your mind, you cannot achieve victory. He was obsessed with sex and porn too and this was his way to fill the lack of professional achievements. This consultation was really interesting, and I tried to explain to him the weaknesses of Vishakha nakshatra and the way he can fix the issues, so he can reach the professional triumph. I am pretty sure, he will succeed...he just needs to find the spiritual hero inside himself and slay the demons of his Ego.

ANURADHA

The Star of Success

ZODIAC RANGE	3°20' SCORPIO - 16°40' SCORPIO
RULING PLANET	SATURN
DEITY	MITRA
SYMBOL	LOTUS FLOWER
CASTE	SHUDRA
ANIMAL	FEMALE DEER
SOUNDS	NA, NEE, NU(NO), NAY
MAIN FIXED STARS	BETA SCORPIONIS, DELTA SCORPIONIS, PI-SCORPIONIS
PADAS	PADA 1- LEO PADA 2- VIRGO PADA 3- LIBRA PADA 4- SCORPIO
COLOR	REDDISH BROWN
GENDER	MALE NAKSHATRA
KEY WORDS	SUCCESS, INSPIRATION, LEADERSHIP, FRIENDSHIP

Meaning

Anuradha is the seventeenth nakshatra in the zodiac belt. It lies entirely in the zodiac sign Scorpio. Anuradha is a mixture of the energies of Scorpio, Mars and Ketu, and Saturn, which is the ruler of this constellation. Scorpio is a dark intense sign, but Anuradha shows us that even in the darkest places, there is still light and hope...all you need is a tiny spark! Saturn teaches the natives of this constellation of responsibility, patience, and restrictions. Saturn will give them the ability to endure all the events in their life.

Anuradha means "After Radha" or "Subsequent Success", some astrologers translate it as "tiny spark". The name "After Radha" connects Anuradha with Vishakha, which alternative name is Radha. So, these two constellations have some common traits. Vishakha is fixation and obsession, while Anuradha is devotion, which is more spiritual, but both constellations are strongly dedicated to something or someone.

The main symbol of Anuradha is a lotus flower. The lotus is one of the most beautiful flowers, but what is interesting is that it grows in dirty swamp waters. Lotus seeds are in the mud, and they are able to grow towards the little sunlight, reach the surface and give one of the most gentle and gorgeous flowers. This fact correlates with the natives of Anuradha – they may face the dark and dirty side of the world, but like the lotus flower, they will be able to rise from the mud and pain and blossom. The roots of this plant are in the muddy ground, where it gets all nutrients, so Anuradha people need to face "the mud" in life to shine and succeed – the pain and struggles are their "nutrients". The other symbol is a staff stick, which is associated with power and protection. Only the biggest sages carry a staff. This symbol is related to knowledge and wisdom, too.

The animal of Anuradha is female deer. Deer is a beautiful, gentle animal. It is associated with the Moon god, who is riding a deer. The animal is mentioned in different Hindu myths, one of them you already know – The Golden deer and Sita.

Deity

The ruling deity of Anuradha is **Mitra**- the God of friendship, good faith, and cordiality. He is one of the solar deities -Adityas. Mitra translates into "friend". Mitra is lighthearted, warm, and friendly and helps us to get rid of the darkness by giving us light. Mitra brings all people together, there is a need to give and receive affection.

He is often invoked with Varuna and Aryaman. Anuradha is one of the most friendly nakshatras. In this constellation love brings together and acts like an inspiration – love not only between lovers but between friends, and between people. Mitra is the divine friend and maintains close alliances and ever-lasting friendships. Bhaga was blinded by Rudra during Daksha sacred fire ceremony, but through the eyes of Mitra, Bhaga was able to view sacrificial offerings. This shows us the kind nature of Mitra and his ability to help others.

Another deity associated with Anuradha is Radha, who was in deep love with Lord Krishna. This love is a high form of devotion. Anuradha is not only getting in touch with the divine but it is associated with enormous love and affection that become devotion.

Since Anuradha is concerned with learning and knowledge, we can associate Saraswati, the Goddess of learning, with this constellation, too.

Key Points

1. All Saturn-ruled nakshatras give prosperity, comfort, and joy and they are benefic for the natives.

2. Anuradha natives can be the best friends. If you need someone to help you, they will be the one. Friendship is really important for these people, sometimes it can be even more important than their family. These natives are kind, friendly, and warm. Please keep in mind that if there is a malefic influence, the result will be the opposite, and this is valid for all nakshatras.

3. Due to mythology Anuradha natives may fall in love with the same person that one of their friends likes or have a sexual affair with. Or they will have a situation when someone breaks up with them, then this person will go to someone else and then come back to the natives. This is due to the story of Varuna and Mitra, who have fallen in love with Urvashi. However, Urvashi liked Mitra more.

4. Anuradha people may have an interest in Greek and Persian culture.

5. Anuradha natives may face a lot of struggles and battles, but this will help them to succeed in life and blossom- they always grew up in harsh dirty environments and rise from mud as lotus.

6. Anuradha people have a strong connection with the divine powers – extremely good astrologers, and numerologists! They are very intelligent and like learning new things. They love music, too.

7. These people can have traits of a deer – they can be very beautiful, youthful, and gracious. They can be very sexual, too. They love to travel and move around. I remember that my astrology teachers told me that all natives, who have prominent

nakshatras ruled by deer animals should be careful when they drive – there can be car accidents. This comes from the fact that deer are frequently hit by cars. The other thing about deer-ruled nakshatras is that they can be the best runners.

8. Anuradha natives can love very deeply and devotedly. Love is important in this constellation. Due to the myth of Radha and Krishna, these people may fall in love with a person that they cannot have. Anuradha natives will always have a bleeding pain in their hearts for not having that person. They can even lose their mind. Anuradha people can love someone till their death.

9. Anuradha individuals have the great ability to gather people together for social activities.

10.   Scorpio can make these people obsessive and jealous. They may look for truth and oppose the old norms and values. Anuradha people like all Scorpio nakshatras are associated with transformation and change. Ego and winning play an important role here.

11.   Due to the mythology associated with Mitra, most Anuradha natives will spend a lot of time alone at some point in their lives. They are curious people, and this quality makes them travel a lot, especially to foreign lands. Anuradha people usually end up settling in faraway places from their birth location.

12.   Anuradha natives are very goal-oriented and focused. However, unlike Vishakha which achieves its goals through power, Anuradha will accomplish through the network of friends and alliances. But like Vishakha, they are willing to go to any length to get their goals.

13.   Since Mitra is always accompanied by Varuna in his adventures, it is commonly seen that the Anuradha natives prefer working with a partner and feel more comfortable being married than being single. You can have a karmic relationship with someone with Shatabisha nakshatra.

14.   Anuradha natives either have a great interest in the plumbing field or always have to deal with plumbing issues in life. This is associated with the stem of the lotus flower that reaches like a pipe the mud in the water.

15.   Anuradha native gains through friendship or some suggestion by a friend.

16.   Anuradha natives are fortunate but acquire all the wealth in the late part of their life - after the age of 48.

17.   Anuradha natives may run into partners who are crazy or obsessed with them, and in marriage, they sometimes end up with a spouse who is jealous and protective. Radha got crazy about Krishna.

18.   Anuradha people are good at research, finance, negotiation, occult, and psychology.

19.   Due to the staff symbol, Anuradha natives love wizards and playing sports that have a stick like golf for example.

20.   Anuradha people can be seen to be founders and leaders of organizations.

Remedies

The best remedy for this nakshatra is to have a statue of a lotus or a deer in your home. The other thing that you have to be very careful with is the plumbing in the house – if you have a problem with the water pipes, you should fix it immediately. Any type of plumbing leak will bring bad luck to you and your house!

Careers/Hobbies

Anuradha nakshatra may produce professions (or hobbies) related to:

- Occult, astrology, psychology, spirituality
- Finance, taxes, negotiations, hidden wealth
- Traveling and everything related to foreigners
- All professions related to groups of people and group activities.
- Plumbing and related professional fields
- Statistics and numbers
- Professions associated with taking care of others and society.
- Research

Examples

I will give you again example with one of my clients.

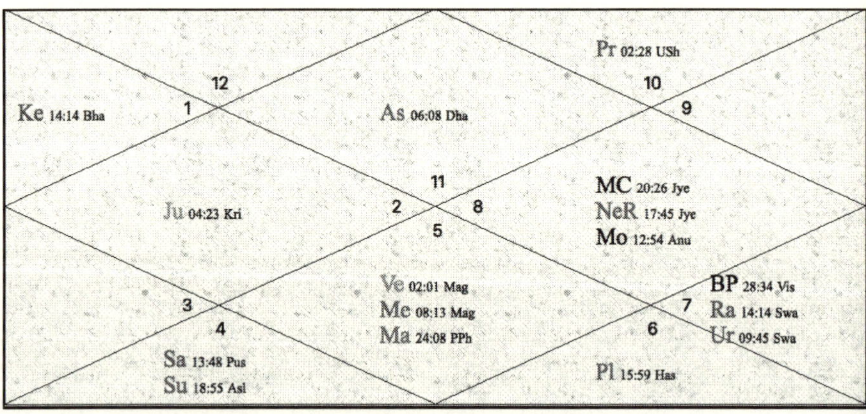

This individual is Aquarius Ascendant and has Moon in Anuradha nakshatra. Moon is debilitated in Scorpio and doesn't feel happy. The Moon is in the house of career, and he was working in the field of finance and taxes, but he had a big interest in astrology- all of that is manifestation of Anuradha. He knew a lot about Western Astrology and came to me for a consultation because he wanted to know more about his Vedic natal chart and what is the difference between both astrological systems

The other manifestation of Anuradha is that he lives far away from his homeland due to his job.

JYESHTA

The Elder (Chief) Star

ZODIAC RANGE	16°40' SCORPIO - 30°00' SCORPIO
RULING PLANET	MERCURY
DEITY	INDRA
SYMBOL	UMBRELLA
CASTE	FARMER
ANIMAL	MALE DEER
SOUNDS	NO, YA, WY, YO
MAIN FIXED STARS	ALPHA SCORPIONIS, SIGMA SCORPIONIS, TAU-SCORPIONIS
PADAS	PADA 1- SAGITTARIUS PADA 2- CAPRICORN PADA 3- AQUARIUS PADA 4- PISCES
COLOR	CREAM
GENDER	FEMALE NAKSHATRA
KEY WORDS	WEALTH, COURAGE, THE CHIEF

Meaning

Jyeshta is the eighteenth nakshatra in the zodiac belt. It lies entirely in the zodiac sign of Scorpio. Jyeshta is a mixture of the energies of Scorpio, Mars and Ketu, and Mercury, which is the ruler of this nakshatra. Mercury and Mars are enemies in Vedic astrology and this can bring a lot of struggles of the mind and verbal aggressiveness, however, this combination can make the natives brave and deep thinkers and philosophers, who fight for the truth and want to know everything about the hidden world. If there is malefic influence, the mix of Scorpion and Mercurial energy can produce one of the biggest manipulators and fraudsters. In this constellation, there is a big battle between the material and spiritual world. Jyeshta is the most intense and deepest part of Scorpio – here, you will feel Mars and Ketu traits in higher doses!

Jyeshta means "the eldest", "the chief", and "the most excellent", some translate it as a "middle finger". We associate the eldest and the chief with respect, honor, wisdom, and knowledge gained from life's lessons. In Indian culture the middle finger is associated with spirituality, kundalini energy, and destiny, however, in the Western world, we associate it with insult and anger. Both aspects of the middle finger can be seen in the Jyeshta natives....they can be spiritual and calm, but they can be rude and unpredictable, too.

The symbol of this nakshatra is an umbrella or talisman or earring. In the different astrology sources, you will find one of these symbols, associated with the nakshatra. The umbrella and the talisman are connected to protection – protection from the physical world around and protection from the occult, unseen world. The umbrella saves you from the rain and the talisman saves you from bad luck. The earring is associated with status and power, both material and spiritual.

The animal of Jyeshta is the male deer, which relates this nakshatra to another deer-ruled nakshatra - Anuradha. The difference is that the Jyeshta deer is male and have antlers. So the deer here is not only beautiful, gracious, fast and always moving and searching for food, but he can be dangerous and attack you if it feels threatened. The change of the deer antlers is connected to transformation and change.

In Jyeshta, you can find one malefic fixed star, called Alpha Scorpionis, also known as Antares or "The rival of Mars". Antares is placed around 16° Scorpio and brings violence and destruction.

Jyeshta, especially in the last degrees (gandanta point), can bring a lot of psychological and physical blocks, and emotional issues. Natives should find their way to spirituality in order to overcome the blocks.

Deity

The ruling deity of Jyeshta is **Indra**, the King of the Gods and God of Wars and Rain. Indra is the co-ruler of Vishakha, which means that all the traits and mythological stories associated with Indra will be significant for Jyeshta, too – all the insecurities, vain character, lavish lifestyle, lust for pleasures and Soma will be valid here. The difference is that Jyeshta is more controlled and secretive than Vishakha.

Indra is considered the hero of the god. He is riding the Airavat elephant, which has 3 trunks. His weapon is the powerful thunderbolt, Vajra.

Indra means "celestial drop" and he is associated with rain. In the past, Indra was one of the most worshipped Gods, because rain is crucial for agriculture, animals, and the life of the planet Earth. As the rain makes the crop grows, so Jyeshta makes its natives grow prosperous. However, very often Jyeshta people will need to turn to spirituality and the occult to get this prosperity – Indra always achieves his victories after occult activity or ceremony.

Indra loves pleasures and likes to get "drunk" by drinking Soma. He steals the nectar from his father and likes to dance after drinking it. He has many sexual encounters. Similarly, Jyeshta natives have passionate and aggressive response toward lovemaking and like to dominate. They can get obsessive at times about sexuality and infidelity and like Indra can frequently commit adultery.

Key Points

1. Jyeshta natives are "the chief" and "the eldest", which means that they can reach the top of their careers and be successful. Attaining the leadership position and making plans for how to achieve it is often seen in this constellation.

2. They can be the eldest sibling in their family or the person, who takes care of the others and be considered as "the eldest one".

3. Jyeshta people should always pay attention to the spiritual world and not let the material world overtakes them.

4. Jyeshta people, like Vishakha, may have a lot of insecurities. They will want to live in beautiful homes, have pleasures, and live a lavish rich life, full of luxuries. These people want the best in life!

5. Jyeshta natives want to win over their enemies at any cost- same as the deity Indra, they don't want to lose their kingdom and status! If they see competition, Jyeshta people will try to

destroy it – ruin the image of the competitors, blackmail them, corrupt others, etc.

6. These people may have mental and emotional blocks and problems with Ego.

7. Jyeshta people, like Indra, are very sexual. They can seduce another person's spouse. They can chase and stalk others.

8. Due to the myth of the 1000 eyes[3] on Indra, Jyeshta natives can be great spies, detectives, and police officers. These natives can be very good at occult, astrology, and tantra.

9. Jyeshta people have a lot of secrets and a strong connection to the underworld. Jyeshta and Magha are the constellations that are connected to the mafia.

10. These people can be very passionate and aggressive – they will first hit, then think.

11. Jyeshta natives may love drinking energy drinks like Red Bull and may love spicy food.

12. Jyeshta natives can be one of the most successful people! They can have fame, power, and wealth, but will always feel insecure. They need to feel superior! Very often these people will have hidden wealth or offshore accounts, many lands, real estates - they like to "hold treasure", to have savings in order to feel safe.

13. Numbers 7 and 49 can play important roles in the life of these natives. This is due to the myth of Indra and Diti. Diti wanted a child, who could destroy Indra. However, Indra sliced the child into 7 pieces, which survived, becoming 7 separate children. Indra sliced them again into another 7 parts, totaling 49. And this is how the

---

[3] Please refer to Vishakha nakshatra

49 Maruts appeared – these are 49 storm deities. Later on, they become friends with Indra. That's why Jyeshta natives can make their enemies friends. This story associate Jyeshta with abortion, too.

14. These people can be very jealous – Jyeshta was the wife of Chandra, who was most jealous of Rohini- Moon's favorite Nakshatra. Therefore, these natives can face jealousy, betrayal, and a sense of abandonment. They can have an enemy with prominent Rohini.

15. The natives demonstrate a sense of seniority and supremacy due to their age and experience.

16. Jyeshta natives may change a lot after a relationship they had. This comes from the animal symbol – the deer loses its antlers after the mating season.

17. Jyeshta people should be careful with their hands, especially their left hand and fingers. This comes from the myth of Indra and Krishna. In order to protect one village from the anger and storms of Indra, Krishna lifted Mount Govardhana and held it for 7 days with his pinky finger on his left hand, creating an umbrella. There can be something specific regarding their nose or face – this is due to the elephant with 3 trunks that Indra rides.

18. The natives are very protective of themselves and their loved ones

19. Jyeshta is also associated with the other qualities of its deity Indra like beauty, bravery and courage, enthusiasm, and energy.

20. This is the nakshatra of war. Jyeshta is the intensified version of Indra. Whenever you think of a man who is rich, an idol, a hero, and loves

to party, you should think of Indra. Most often that individual would have an Indra ruled nakshatra (Vishakha or Jyeshta) in their chart.

Remedies

The best remedy for this nakshatra is to have a deer statue. You should respect the elders, too. If you have a broken umbrella, talisman, or earring, you have to fix it or throw it, because it will bring losses to you.

If you want protection and good luck, you can buy a talisman.

Careers/Hobbies

Jyeshta nakshatra may produce professions (or hobbies) related to:

- Military, police, secret agencies, fire department

- Finance, hidden wealth, tax

- Research and analysis

- Politics, managers, leaders – "chief-s" of all kinds (CEOs -chief executive officers, etc.)

- Governmental and administrative professions

- Professions related to the sports field.

- Occult, astrology, spirituality

- Sex and entertainment industry

- Professions associated with elder people

- Professions related to liquids

Examples

Some of the most famous representatives of Jyeshta nakshatra are Frank Sinatra, Elvis Presley, Tiger Woods, and Al Pacino. As typical Jyeshta natives all of them are considered playboys, who have big fortune, love women, drinking, and fame, same as their God Indra.

Jyeshta is the last nakshatra from the second circle of 9 constellations. The first circle was from Ashwini till Ashlesha and have more Rajas qualities – they want to act and create. The second circle is from Magha till Jyeshta and has more Tamas qualities – focused on the material world. The third circle is from Mula till Revati and has more Sattva qualities – spiritual enlightenment.

MULA

The Foundation Star

ZODIAC RANGE	0°00' SAGITTARIUS - 13°20' SAGITTRIUS
RULING PLANET	KETU
DEITY	NIRITTI
SYMBOL	BUNCH OF ROOTS
CASTE	BUTCHER
ANIMAL	MALE DOG
SOUNDS	YEH, YO, BA, BE
MAIN FIXED STARS	SHAULA, LESATH AND STARS CONNECTED TO THE CENTER OF THE MILKY WAY GALAXY
PADAS	PADA 1- ARIES PADA 2- TAURUS PADA 3- GEMINI PADA 4- CANCER
COLOR	BRIGHT YELLOW
GENDER	MALE NAKSHATRA
KEY WORDS	DESTRUCTION, CHANGE, INQUIRING, INTELLIGENT

Meaning

Mula is the nineteenth nakshatra in the zodiac belt. It lies entirely in the zodiac sign of Sagittarius. Mula is a combination of the energies and traits of Sagittarius, its ruler Jupiter and the ruler of the nakshatra- Ketu.

What is Sagittarius? Sagittarius is associated with gurus, teachers, preachers, philosophers, religion, and higher knowledge. It rules spirituality, laws, temples, different cultures, and long-distance traveling. Sagittarius brings expansion and optimism. Jupiter and Ketu make this nakshatra extremely spiritual and philosophical. Ketu is an indicator of spiritual enlightenment, unfortunately on this planet, the attaining of moksha comes through pain, struggles, and destruction of the old self. Ketu is the past, so you should learn well the lessons from your past.

Mula is another heavy and difficult nakshatra. As I have mentioned before, I have noticed in my horoscope reading consultations, that clients, who have prominent Bharani, Ardra, and Mula nakshatras face a lot of pain, dissatisfaction, and transformation in life. Whenever Rahu and Ketu transit over Ardra and Mula, there are catastrophic events that shutter the world and give us signs that we need to change! Ketu is one of the most dangerous planets for the material realm – it detaches you from everything material, cleansing your soul, and destroying you, so it can build another version of you. Mula not only has destructive tendencies, but it has self-destructive inclinations, too. If there is a malefic influence, there can be suicide or self-harm.

Mula translates to "the roots", and "the center". This constellation goes directly to the core of things, to the bottom, to the center. Mula people are straightforward and go directly to the roots of life and the problems, they are facing. The Mula constellation is located in the center of the Milky Way and as per Vedic astrology, this center is considered one of the most powerful spiritual points. This is the reason why Vedic scholars accept Mula as the most spiritual nakshatra.

The symbol of Mula is a bunch of roots. Both name and symbol emphasize on the word "roots", so in Mula the roots, literally and figuratively, are crucial! Roots are hidden, so that's why this constellation deals with the hidden world, and hidden events, it investigates everything unseen and unknown. Mula natives need to remember the importance of their family roots and traditions. Mula is connected to Ayurveda and healing. In order to heal, you will need to take the old roots out and plant new ones. There is a theme of rooting out the old version of you to become a better and happier person. The process of uprooting is painful.

The animal of Mula is a male dog. It is connected to the dog of Bhairava, which is standing next to Lord Shiva. Dogs can be aggressive and wild, but they can be trained and become people's best friends. In Mula, it is important to tame your inner beast and self-discipline yourself.

Deity

The ruling deity of Mula is **Nirriti**, the Goddess of death and destruction. She is also called Alakshmi or the opposite of Lakshmi, who is the goddess of prosperity. Nirriti is the mother of Mrithyu, which is death, Bhaya, which is fear, and MahaBhaya, which is terror. She is the daughter of Adharma, which is unrighteousness, and Himsa, which is violence. The deity confirms again that Mula is one of the most difficult nakshatras.

Nirriti is associated with misfortune and poverty. It is related to Goddess Kali. Kali is death, darkness, and violence. This goddess is associated with the black hole in the center of the Milky Way. Kali can grant you eternal life, but there is a price that you need to pay. This is the reason why Mula natives will need to sacrifice something in their life. Please don't think that if you have Mula you will be poor and unhappy, on the contrary- Mula can give you prosperity and high status, but if you don't follow the righteous way and have a spiritual path, you will lose the material prosperity at some point of your life.

Key Points

1. All Ketu nakshatras have incredible healing abilities. Mula natives can be experts in herbs, Ayurveda, and medicine in general. They can become great doctors and healers. These natives are good at occult, astrology, and tantra. They can have extreme spiritual powers.

2. Mula is one of the most difficult nakshatras – its natives may face pain, dissatisfaction, and destruction in different forms in order to clean their souls and find their way to the spiritual world. They will need to pay attention to their roots and root out everything that they don't need anymore. There is a theme of sacrifice in their life.

3. Mula natives are profound personalities – they are not superficial and go to the center of the issue, go to the roots of everything. They try to refine everything, too. Mula natives are the embodiment of their roots, their past, and their ancestors.

4. Mula natives, together with Ardra, can be the most loyal friends and spouses. Mula natives can get attached to someone very easily.

5. Mula people will need to destroy the old in order new things to grow in their life. Their deity is

Nirriti – the Goddess of Destruction, so they can have her destructive powers. They can be violent, cruel, unpredictable, and mad. They can have interests in the underworld, unseen things, cemeteries, graves, occult, skeletons, cremation, and everything that is under the ground. Mula natives may seek consolation in black magic- casting spells on others, exorcism, punishments, and even murder.

6. Mula people love history, archeology, and ancient worlds

7. Mula natives may love eating plants that grow underground- carrot, ginger, beet, potatoes, etc.

8. Love the smell of the smoke of fire and cigarettes. They can be addicted to smoking, alcohol, or drugs.

9. These natives may be interested in the universe, galaxies, planets, etc.

10. Mula and Uttara Ashadha natives love desserts and places with sand.

11. They may have strange or unaccepted sexual relationships. According to some texts, Nirriti marries her brother Anrta, and they have children.

12. Mula is connected to Kali - the fierce goddess who wears a necklace of skulls and human heads. Her dance destroys illusions and helps us see reality. Mula natives will be able to show us the truth and destroy the illusions. However, they should be careful with their heads literally and figuratively – not only because Kali had a necklace with human heads, but because Ketu is "a body without a head". In other myths, Nirriti plunked out of

the anus, so natives should be careful with this region, too.

13. Mula natives are good at organizing, putting in order, and tying together things.

14. These natives may face difficult events, especially in their early childhood.

15. Mula natives can be very successful and wealthy, however, there can be extreme reversals in their lives, which may bring losses. Ketu teaches them the lesson of non-attachment to the material world.

16. Mula natives may love fig trees (Peepal tree)- this is due to the mythology of Lakshmi and her sister Alakshimi. Lakshmi visited her elder sister every Saturday on the Peepal tree. Mula natives pay respect to their elder siblings.

17. Some astrologers connect Mula with the Blackholes in the Universe – they describe them as mysterious, dangerous, and crushing everything on their way, sucking the energy and life. That is why Mula natives may love crushing things – like cans for example, or watch news related to crashes and it can be difficult to stay around Mula people- they can suck your energy.

Remedies

The best remedy for this nakshatra is to go out and plant a flower or tree outside in the garden or the park. If you have issues with love, you can plant a rose. It is recommended to eat vegetables that grow under the ground.

You can read books about the cosmos, galaxies, Milky Way, and black holes, but please keep in mind that if you have spiritual books, they have to be in good shape – if they are torn or missing pages, it is better to remove them from your house.

The other remedy is to have a dog.

Careers/Hobbies

Mula nakshatra may produce professions (or hobbies) related to:

- Occult and spirituality
- Professions associated with psychology, counseling, and coaching.
- Research and investigation
- Professions associated with plants and agriculture
- Professions associated with destruction and cleansing, death
- Healing and medicine
- Professions related to everything under the ground – oil, gas, gems, diamonds, gold, coal, etc.
- Teaching and Speaking
- Cosmos and galaxies

Examples

I will give you one example with one of my clients. This individual came for detailed horoscope reading. He was very interested in astrology and wanted to know more about his destiny and what is his mission in this life.

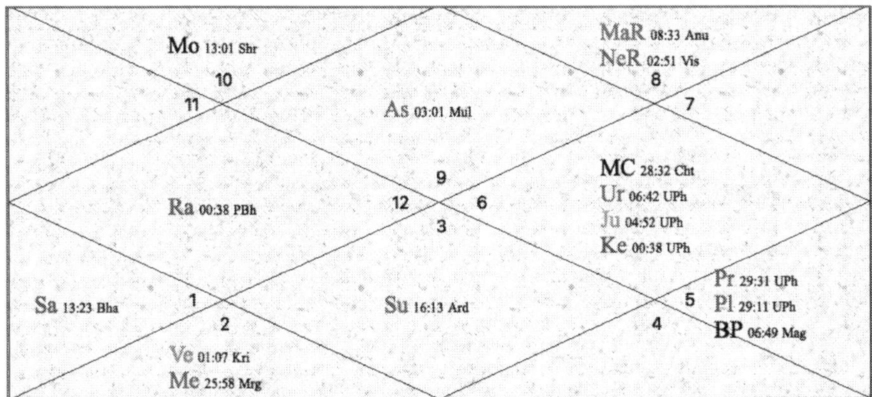

My client has an Ascendant in Mula. The first manifestation of this nakshatra was that he loves ginger and beetroot. He is into herbs and wants to develop in the field of Ayurveda and herbalism. And the most interesting thing is that he has a dog, called Milky !!! This was a really funny manifestation – the dog is a symbol of the nakshatra and Mula is placed in the center of the Milky Way.

PURVA ASHADHA

The Invincible Star

ZODIAC RANGE	13°20' SAGITTARIUS - 26°40' SAGITTRIUS
RULING PLANET	VENUS
DEITY	APAS
SYMBOL	FAN
CASTE	BRAHMIN
ANIMAL	MALE MONKEY
SOUNDS	BU, DHA, PHA, DHAA
MAIN FIXED STARS	EPSILON SAGITTARI, DELTA SAGITTARI, LAMBDA SAGITTARI
PADAS	PADA 1- LEO PADA 2- VIRGO PADA 3- LIBRA PADA 4- SCORPIO
COLOR	BLACK
GENDER	FEMALE NAKSHATRA
KEY WORDS	INVINCIBLE, VICTORY, TRAVELLING OVER WATER

Meaning

Purva Ashadha is the twentieth nakshatra in the zodiac belt. It lies entirely in the zodiac sign of Sagittarius. Purva Ashadha is a mixture of the energies of Sagittarius, Jupiter, and Venus, which is the ruler of this nakshatra. Venus is the guru of demons and an enemy of Jupiter, who is the guru of Gods – there is a big rivalry between them, which can be seen in the traits of the natives of this constellation. Here, Venus bestows not only interest in spirituality and knowledge but many artistic and creative talents.

Purva Ashadha means "Early victory", "The former invincible one" or "the undefeated", which indicates that this nakshatra cannot be conquered or suppressed. Victory plays an important role here. The main symbol of this nakshatra is a fan. The fan can be used for multiple reasons- in the past, it was a symbol of social status, fame, talents, and creative expression. Of course, nowadays it has a more practical side – cooling yourself or hiding your face. Alternative symbols of this constellation are elephant tusk and winnowing basket. The elephant tusk is dangerous – it can kill, still it is beautiful and precious, too. The winnowing basket is a basket used to winnow rice or grain from the chaff, so we connect this symbol with judging and checking the quality of things, evaluating things. The animal of Purva Ashadha is a male monkey. Monkeys are clever, amusing, brave, and sometimes irritating – so all of these characteristics can be seen in Purva Ashadha natives. In Vedic culture, monkeys are associated with Hanuman and the vanaras, who are monkeys with powers. Hanuman is seen in multiple stories with Vishnu, and Shiva, he was a devotee of Rama and helped him in the search for his wife Sita, who was kidnapped by a demon. Purva Ashadha can develop great loyalty, a desire to help and fight against injustice.

This nakshatra is associated with declarations of war. One of the reasons for that is because the planet Mars is born in this constellation.

Deity

The ruling deity of Purva Ashadha is **Apas**, the Goddess of cosmic waters. Apas is considered to be the wife of Varuna, the God of oceans. Water is extremely powerful – it is a source of life- without it, the Earth and life cannot exist. Water can clean the body and can cleanse the soul, it can represent purity and cleaning of the sins, so that's why water is used in many religious ceremonies. Purva Ashadha can be connected to cleaning the people of their sins, so they can accomplish the purpose of their life.

Like the waters, Purva Ashadha nakshatra is easily stirred and agitated. It can make us easily excited and enthusiastic about something.

Apas can be associated with Aphrodite and sea creatures like mermaids. This makes Purva Ashadha natives very mysterious, beautiful, vain, talented, and free. Other gods linked to Apas are Varuna, Soma, Indra, and Agni – all connected through the element of water.

Purva Ashadha has the qualities of the water. Water is strong enough to destroy rocks, yet it can be soft, too. Like the water is spreading in different directions, same the name and reputation of the natives of this constellation can spread, too – that's why they can become famous and recognized.

Key Points

1. Purva Ashadha natives are undefeatable- they want to win and be famous and recognized. They want to have a status in society, wealth,

comfort, and the best of everything – the best cars, best brands, flying first class, etc. These natives are very independent, and they can be great leaders. They can be fearless, aggressive, confrontational, egoistic, and controlling toward achieving their goals. These natives may fight against injustice. Their success will come at an early age

2. Purva Ashadha people have a strong devotion to the guru, higher philosophy, and teacher. Devotion to someone and something can be seen in the life of these people, due to their association with Hanuman. They always bring value to other people's life.

3. Purva Ashadha natives have the qualities of the water – they can be soft, they can be destructive, too. They have the ability to purify things that are impure. Water gives life – so they can be very "fertile" individuals. Water changes forms- so natives can be very adaptable and good at transformations.

4. These natives like fans, so you will see them turning on the air conditioning constantly.

5. These natives can be very social – they like interacting with others.

6. Purva Ashadha natives can be great teachers – they can teach everything in a simple way.

7. These natives cannot stick to one thing for too long – they are like monkeys, jumping from one branch to another. They need freelance jobs or work on projects, otherwise, they can get and lose their jobs all the time.

8. These people have great strategic skills. They can be very proud, and they can influence the masses. They have great oratory abilities and

are good debaters- they can defeat anyone in an argument. This nakshatra is associated with declarations of war, so their attitude is a bit angry and sharp.

9. Purva Ashadha natives love water, and they can do business in fields, associated with water. They love traveling, especially to places near oceans and seas.

10. Purva Ashadha natives are intelligent and can be great gurus. There is a philosophical and emotional depth in these people. Venus brings here love for music, art, and sensual side of life. Purva Ashadha natives have a strong procreative and sexual drive, which is why they are lucky to attract a loving spouse and good friends in life. They can gain prosperity through women.

11. Purva Ashadha natives have a strong need to always better their life or improve their situation, they want to climb higher in society.

12. These people have the ability to judge good from bad, positive from negative. They make good choices that enhance their lives.

13. My Vedic teachers always mentioned that these people have issues in education – there can be dropping out of school/ university, obstacles in graduating, etc.

14. Purva Ashadha natives love watching, reading or writing about wars and battles.

15. These natives can accomplish the most challenging and unimaginable tasks with their cleverness and strategic intelligence.

Remedies

The best remedy for this nakshatra is to live around the water or travel to resorts next to water. You can have some rituals with water, too – or at least drink a lot of water, nice tea or have a day only of drinking water every few weeks, depending on your health.

Purva Ashadha people should take care of their teeth.

You can take a statue of a monkey or Hanuman.

Careers/Hobbies

Purva Ashadha nakshatra may produce professions (or hobbies) related to:

- All professions linked to water and liquids
- Tourism and travel industry
- Managers and leaders of all types, politicians
- War, battles, defense, arguments, debates
- Professions associated with art and creativity
- Gurus, teachers, preachers, speakers, and orators
- Spirituality and knowledge
- Body and fitness; cleaning

Examples

One of the most famous representatives of Purva Ashadha is Hitler. He had his Moon in this nakshatra. He was a leader and politician, and he was the one who caused the Second World War. He had amazing oratory skills and was able to control and influence the masses, unfortunately, for bad causes, not for the betterment of humanity.

UTTARA ASHADHA

The Universal Star

ZODIAC RANGE	26°40' SAGITTARIUS - 10°00' CAPRICORN
RULING PLANET	SUN
DEITY	VISHWADEVAS
SYMBOL	ELEPHANT TUSK
CASTE	WARRIOR
ANIMAL	MALE MONGOOSE
SOUNDS	BE, BA, JA, JE
MAIN FIXED STARS	NUNKI, ASCELLA, ALBADAH, TAU SAGITTARI
PADAS	PADA 1- SAGITTARIUS PADA 2- CAPRICORN PADA 3- AQUARIUS PADA 4- PISCES
COLOR	COPPER
GENDER	FEMALE NAKSHATRA
KEY WORDS	GREAT, AMBITIOUS, POWER, HONEST

Meaning

Uttara Ashadha is the twenty-first nakshatra in the zodiac belt. It overlaps two zodiac signs – starts at 26°40' Sagittarius and ends at 10° Capricorn. Sagittarius and Capricorn are two completely different energies. In the first part of the nakshatra, you feel the energies of Sagittarius, Jupiter, and the Sun, which is the ruler of the constellation. In the second part, you feel the energies of Capricorn, Saturn, and the Sun.

What is Capricorn? Capricorn is the natural tenth zodiac sign and is associated with profession, authority, leaders, government, status, fame, life path and purpose. It is practical, serious, hardworking, and conservative. It is related to slow but steady progress, structures, organizations, and delays, too.

The Sagittarius part of Uttara Ashadha is more spiritual, while the Capricorn part is more material and practical. Sun and Saturn are enemies in Vedic Astrology, so for sure there will be a complicated relationship regarding power, success, and leadership. Sun signifies authority and power and will bestow Uttara Ashadha natives with skills to command and influence other people. However, the Capricorn natives of this nakshatra can become more strict and harsh leaders and it can be difficult to work with such people. Jupiter is debilitated in Capricorn.

Uttara Ashadha means "the latter invincible one", "later victory", and "the latter undefeated" and it is connected with the previous nakshatra -Purva Ashadha. They have some similar traits. Uttara Ashadha is the final victory- the one that wins officially the war, not only the battle. Sometimes winners are lonely...people who have succeeded and reached the top of their fields are loners. So, Uttara Ashadha is associated with loneliness.

The symbol of Uttara Ashadha is an elephant tusk or a plank of a bed. The tusks are one of the most precious parts of the elephants, they are even killed for their tusks. This symbol represents royal status, power, strength, danger, and leadership. Both Purva and Uttara Ashadha are connected to aggressive actions, including the declaration of war. Purva's alternative symbol is again a tusk of the elephant. Some astrologers say that Purva is the left tusk and Uttara Ashadha is the right tusk of the elephant. The other symbol is a plank of a bed. This bed is not the same as the bed that we discussed in Purva and Uttara Phalguni. Uttara Ashadha's bed is harsher, without any comfort. It signifies giving up luxury and material desires.

The animal of the nakshatra is a male mongoose. Uttara Ashadha is the only nakshatra that doesn't have an animal pair! This is again associated with loneliness and independence. My Atmakaraka is in this nakshatra in my birth chart, and I can confirm that you feel lonely, and it is very difficult to connect with people sometimes. You can be surrounded by hundreds of people, but deep inside you still feel lonely. We have to take into consideration the other part of the birth chart – this is not valid for all Uttara Ashadha natives, of course. The mongoose is connected with Kubera, the god of wealth. He is illustrated as a dwarf that holds a mongoose in his hand. Mongoose is a victory against Nagas, who keep the treasures. Uttara Ashadha wants to kill the snakes and remove the poison and the old karma.

Uttara Ashadha nakshatra is less self-oriented than Purva Ashadha. Both constellations are undefeatable, but Uttara lacks the softness of the water, so it can be more rude and harsh in some ways.

Deity

The ruling deity of Uttara Ashadha is the Universal Gods, also known as **Vishvadevas**. Viswadevas deals with universal moral principles. These deities are the 10 sons of God Dharma – Vasu (Goodness), Satya (Truth), Kratu (Willpower), Daksha (Ritual skills), Kala (Time), Kama (Desires), Dhriti (Forbearance), Kuru (Ancestors), Puraravas (Abundance), Madrava (Joy). They grant the natives the final victory. They are benefic deities, which represent the good in the world.

Ganesha is another deity associated with this constellation. Ganesha is the god of beginnings, which is why Uttara Ashadha relates to all types of new beginnings.

Key Points

1. All Sun-ruled nakshatra want to change society for the better. Uttara Ashadha is the highest Sun nakshatra and it is the highest of your Dharma – life purpose. These natives want to help people and change the world for the better. They see people as equal no matter their race, gender, or sexual orientation. They can be great leaders and politicians. They can be extremely influential and control the masses. However, this is a nakshatra where wars are declared, so it can be quite aggressive.

2. Uttara Ashadha can produce great writers, especially in the field of politics and society. This is associated with a myth about Lord Ganesha who broke his tusk and turned it into a pen. Ganesha wrote Mahabharata. These natives may love reading or watching trilogy movies, or books.

3. Uttara Ashadha natives can be lonely– the mongoose is the only animal without a partner in the animal classification of the nakshatras. These people will search for the perfect partner

and will feel lonely, no matter how many people surround them. Mongooses eat snakes, so these people may hate snakes and reptiles or the traits that snakes symbolize in humans. They can have enemies with Ashlesha and Mrigashira nakshatras. Mongooses live in groups, so these natives will create their group of people. Mongooses are smelly animals, so the natives will use many perfumes and deodorants. Uttara Ashadha natives, like the mongooses, are courageous, clever and go ahead in difficult and dangerous situations.

4. Uttara Ashadha people are very opportunistic and grab every chance they have.

5. These natives always have a Muslim friend - mongoose is around warthogs (pigs), which is symbolized by Rahu – Rahu is associated with Muslims, Ketu with Buddhists, so Uttara Ashadha have Muslim friends or marry a Muslim, or they will get opportunities through Muslims

6. Before the age of 33, these people will have a lot of obstacles and struggles, after that age, they will start gradually to grow and prosper. Since this nakshatra means "Late victory", these natives will fully succeed after the age of 38.

7. Uttara Ashadha natives have similar traits to Purva Ashadha natives – they want victory, they want to reach the top of their careers, and have a successful life. The victory here includes uniting the people and society, not dividing it. Uttara natives search for the truth. They are wanderers with many friends and foes.

8. These people love history, colonial history, love colonial homes, homes like churches, castle.

9. Uttara Ashadha natives like to command other people, they are workaholics, very competitive and seek great achievements. They don't trust other people completely. They fight for what they believe is right, very righteous and responsible people. They practice what they preach. Uttara natives are sincere, and they seldom lie.

10. Uttara natives can be very good teachers and counselors.

11. Uttara Ashadha natives fall in love with the intellect and qualities of other people, especially the ones they are dating. Natives may fall in love with an unmarried woman/man.

12. It is noticed that at the end of every activity, Uttara Ashadha natives expect appreciation from others as it boosts their ego and motivates them to take another responsibility. It is seen that their high ethics, morals, and ideals usually get them into trouble in society

13. They may have deep respect for traditions and their ancestors.

14. The influence of the Saturn in Capricorn part of this nakshatra can give a rigid nature, that doesn't show any tolerance towards anything which does not follow the normal respectable lines.

15. Uttara Ashadha respects all religions and believes in the Universal God.

16. Uttara Ashadha natives should be careful with their legs, knee, and ankles. This comes from the myth that Krishna was killed by an arrow on his left foot. They have to be careful with their teeth, too, especially if there is a malefic influence.

17.   Uttara Ashadha natives come to change things, and they make a big impact on society. They will need to lose many early battles, to win the final one.

Remedies

The best remedy for this nakshatra is to have a beautiful statue of an elephant. The other remedy is to check your teeth and take care of them all the time.

It is recommended these people believe in something bigger than them....atheists cannot have the final victory!

It is said that smoking cigars and wearing beautiful wristwatches will bring good luck to the natives.

Careers/Hobbies

Uttara Ashadha nakshatra may produce professions (or hobbies) related to:

- Military and defense

- Spirituality, religion, and astrology

- Psychology

- Politicians, leaders, and authorities of all types

- Government

- Lawyers and judges

- Teachers

- Athletes

Examples

I will give you an example with one of my clients

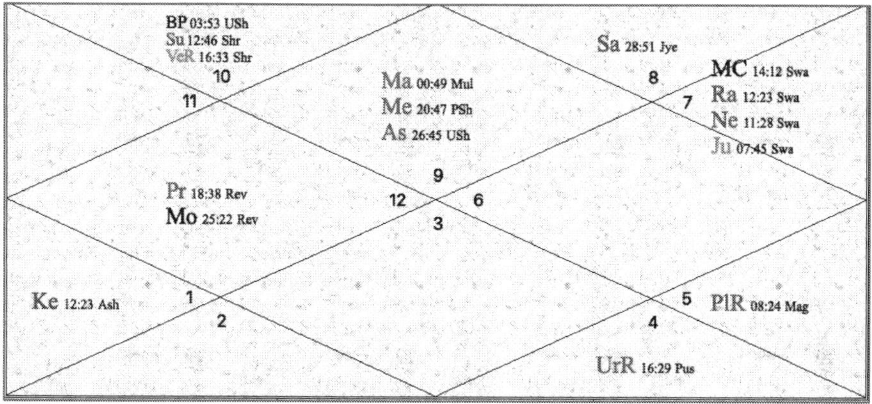

This client booked a yearly horoscope reading with me. He has his Ascendant in Uttara Ashadha. He was working as a counselor and psychologist, which can be the typical career for this nakshatra, the other thing is he had a strict value system and, to be honest, he didn't agree a lot with the concepts, which don't match his values. Another interesting manifestation is that he had a statue of Ganesha in his home, and he was unmarried.

SHRAVANA

The Star of learning

ZODIAC RANGE	10°00' CAPRICORN – 23°20' CAPRICORN
RULING PLANET	MOON
DEITY	VISHNU
SYMBOL	AN EAR
CASTE	OUTCAST
ANIMAL	FEMALE MONKEY
SOUNDS	JU, JAY, JO, GHA
MAIN FIXED STARS	ALTAIR, ALSHAIN, TARAZED
PADAS	PADA 1- ARIES PADA 2- TAURUS PADA 3- GEMINI PADA 4- CANCER
COLOR	LIGHT BLUE
GENDER	MALE NAKSHATRA
KEY WORDS	LEARNING, TEACHING, LISTENING, SPEAKING

Meaning

Shravana is the twenty-second nakshatra in the zodiac belt. It lies entirely in the zodiac sign Capricorn. Shravana is a mixture of the energies of the Capricorn, Saturn, and the Moon, which is the ruler of this nakshatra. It is a little bit surprising that this gentle planet, the Moon, rules a constellation, which is part of the strict and harsh Capricorn. Moon and Saturn are enemies in Vedic Astrology. Moon is the mind and here this mind has to work hard in order to develop. Through constant practice of the mind and all qualities and power that the mind possesses, Shravana natives can grow.

Shravana means "hear/listen" or "the one who limps". Hearing is associated with the process of listening to the teacher, the guru and it is part of the learning. It is important to listen to the divine within, which can bring spiritual enlightenment. When you listen, you have to be silent...so silence is another key word for this nakshatra. "The one who limps" is connected with the story of Vanama and MahaBali and the three steps that Vanama took to conquer again the world of the Gods. The main symbol of this nakshatra is an ear, so in this constellation the ability to listen is crucial. Listening is a part of the whole communication process. The ear is associated with knowledge, learning, teaching, music, and sounds. The animal of Shravana is the female monkey, the same as the animal of Purva Ashadha- the male monkey. Monkeys are clever, brave, funny, curious, vibrant, and sometimes irritating. The difference here, compared to the monkey of Purva Ashadha, is that the female monkey takes care of the learning process of her baby monkeys and brings her baby everywhere with her. So all of these qualities can be seen in the Shravana natives. As you already know, we associate monkeys with Hanuman and the vanaras.

Deity

The ruling deity of Shravana is **Vishnu**. Vishnu is considered one of the most important deities of the Vedas. He is part of the Trimurti, together with Shiva and Brahma. Vishnu is responsible for preserving the world and supporting its creation. It is said that Shravana nakshatra represents the three footprints of Vishnu. The alternative symbol of this nakshatra is 3 steps, again associated with the Vanama myth.

Vishnu can be translated to "that which is everywhere". Vishnu helps our mind to be clear and perceive what we are listening to and gain knowledge. Acquiring knowledge is another key theme for this nakshatra.

Vishnu had multiple incarnations, so he is many beings. Vishnu will reincarnate in this world to protect it. Some of the most famous reincarnations of Vishnu are Varaha, Vanama, Rama, Krishna, and Buddha. So, all of the myths associated with them will be valid for this nakshatra.

Saraswati is another deity, related to Shravana. This makes the Shravana natives good in all fields, involving speech, music, languages, and education.

Key Points

1. Shravana natives should always listen to their inner voice! It is recommended to do meditation and to pay attention to the inner world and what the silence around you, will whisper in your ear. When you don't know what to do, just calm down, sit in silence and meditate – this can give you directions. Of course, it is always good to pay attention to what you are hearing around you and how this resembles your inner world. Every sound, every word, and every noise may

give you information about people, situations, and actions. Generally said Shravana natives must listen to everything carefully, or they can miss some of the most important information, advice, and wisdom in their life. It is said that it's good to listen to your guru, too.

2. Shravana natives can be very good at teaching, singing, playing musical instruments, and speaking languages – all fields related to speaking, hearing, and communication.

3. Due to the myth of Vanama[4], number 3 may play an important role for Shravana natives – they may have 3 houses, and 3 cars, they may change the place of living 3 times or everything they do has to be done 3 times, collecting 3 similar souvenirs, etc. – all depends on the whole birth chart of the natives. They can have success in foreign lands. Shravana natives can look like a small child like Vanama, but inside they can be the powerful Vishnu and achieve great accomplishments. Due to Vanama's myth, they will take someone else spot – if you are in the company, you may take over the position of your team lead or manager.

4. Shravana natives love studying the stars and the cosmos.

5. Shravana natives are natural philanthropists – they care about people and want to nourish them.

6. Shravana natives, like Purva Ashadha natives, have similar qualities to their ruling animal – the monkeys. They are intelligent, brave, funny, curious, and of course irritating. They go from one thing to another – from one branch to

---

[4] Please refer to Punarvasu nakshatra and the myth of Vanama

another. They will move constantly – change their place of living a lot. Shravana natives know how to grab every opportunity.

7. Shravana natives will have a specific way of walking. They may love hiking and biking. They may have a tattoo on their leg.

8. Shravana people are good at mathematics. They may love counting or always say words like 1-2-3 or 3-2-1. They are good at learning through listening.

9. Shravana natives may feel earthquakes before they happen.

10.   Knowledge and education are keywords for Shravana – these people can be extremely intelligent and knowledgeable.

11.   Shravana natives are very sensitive and can get hurt very easily. If influenced by malefic planets, they can suffer from not having been heard. They can feel disregarded and not recognized. There seem to be trouble and disappointments early in life. Problems with the ears can be seen, too.

12.   Shravana is concerned about what people say about them and their public reputation. They are sensitive to the opinions of others.

13.   Shravana natives must listen to their spouse's advice when it involves land, property, or real estate. This is again a result of Vanama's myth.

Remedies

The best remedies for this nakshatra are to buy 3 monkey statues, watch or read trilogies, hike in the mountains, or ride a bike.

The other auspicious thing is to meditate and sit in silence, so you can hear the voice within.

Careers/Hobbies

Shravana nakshatra may produce professions (or hobbies) related to:

- All professions associated with listening, speaking, music, sounds and communication

- All professions related to education and teaching.

- Ears doctor

- Travel industry

- Professions associated with charity

- Professions related to knowledge and skills

Examples

Some of the most famous representatives of Shravana nakshatra are Oprah Winfrey, James Dean, and Bruce Willis.

Oprah Winfrey has her Sun and Venus in Shravana. Oprah is a typical manifestation of this nakshatra – first, she was a TV host, which is related to both listening and speaking. Now she has her own TV channel – which is again related to communication, broadcasting, listening, and speaking. She is famous for her charity and helping society. She even founded schools for women in South Africa – again another important theme for Shravana- the education. Oprah became something like a "spiritual teacher" for others and if you have watched her motivational videos on YouTube, she often speaks about listening to the inner voice and signal of the Universe.

DHANISHTA

The Star of Symphony

ZODIAC RANGE	23°20' CAPRICORN – 6°40' AQUARIUS
RULING PLANET	MARS
DEITY	THE EIGHT VASUS
SYMBOL	A DRUM
CASTE	WARRIOR
ANIMAL	FEMALE LION
SOUNDS	GA, GE, GO, GAY
MAIN FIXED STARS	ALPHA DELPHINI, BETA DELPHINI, DELTA DELPHINI, GAMMA DELPHINI
PADAS	PADA 1- LEO PADA 2- VIRGO PADA 3- LIBRA PADA 4- SCORPIO
COLOR	SILVER
GENDER	FEMALE NAKSHATRA
KEY WORDS	WEALTH, MUSIC, OPTIMISM

Meaning

Dhanishta is the twenty-third nakshatra in the zodiac belt. It overlaps two zodiac signs – it starts at 23°20' Capricorn and ends at 6°40' Aquarius. In the first part of this nakshatra, you feel the energies of Capricorn, Saturn, and Mars, which is the ruler of this nakshatra. In the second part, you feel the energies of Aquarius, Saturn and Rahu, which are both rulers of the zodiac sign Aquarius, and Mars again.

What is Aquarius? Aquarius is the most eccentric zodiac sign. It is full of ideas, out-of-the-box, awkward, independent, inventive, and scientific. It rules society, social circles, the economy, big organizations, income, New Age, and new technology. Aquarius is the other karmic sign, together with Scorpio.

Mars gives courage and power to the natives of this constellation, especially in the part of Capricorn, where Mars feels exalted. These people are born to conquer their enemies. Both Capricorn and Aquarius are ruled by Saturn, so all the qualities of this planet will be seen in Dhanishta. Capricorn part, figuratively said, is more introverted- it is responsible, hardworking, and practical, while the Aquarius part is more extroverted - more philosophical and society oriented. In Aquarius, the energies are really powerful, and they can create a great battle in the mind of natives – Saturn is delay, Mars is action, Saturn and Mars are enemies, Rahu is unpredictable and wants everything material...so these people will need to learn how to control these powers and if they learn to do that and there is no malefic influence, they can be incredible and invincible.

Dhanishta means "the wealthy one", "the most beneficent". The alternative name of Dhanishta is Shravishta, which means "the most famous". This tells us that Dhanishta is extremely auspicious and can give wealth and fame to the natives. Please note that wealth is not only material, it can be spiritual, too. The symbol of this constellation is a drum, which Vedic scholars associate with Shiva's Mridanga (drum), and Krishna's Bansuri (flute), so this connects Dhanishta with music, sounds, and the ability to connect to the divine rhythm. Dhanishta is called the star of symphony, so the music will play a crucial role here. Vedic astrologers put focus on the fact that the drum is hollow, and the natives will need to "fill" the hollowness with something – dreams, meaning, or life's purpose. I put the focus on the effect of the drum on the other people and how it influences them. The animal of this constellation is a lioness. We associate it with Narasimhi, who is half lion, half woman. She is the wife of Narasimha, who was created by Gods to kill a demon, who conquered their kingdom. Narasimhi had to calm down her spouse after he killed the demon. In the wild nature, the lioness is strong, clever, beautiful, and lives in a big group, pride. They are the engine of the pride, not the male lion. So, Dhanishta natives are typical lionesses.

Deity

The ruling deity of Dhanishta is the **eight Vasus**. Vasus means "superb, excellent". Their names are Apas – water, Dhruva – steady or fixed, associated with the Pole star, Soma – the Moon, Dhara – the bearer, support, earth, Anila -wind, Anala – fire, Pratyusha -dawn, Prabhas – light, sky. The 8 Vasus carry the energies of different nakshatras – so this makes Dhanishta a combination of the qualities of the previous nakshatras. These 8 Vasus are the Gods of abundance and are supposed to be wealthy and skilled in music.

There is one myth, which will help you understand one of the traits of the constellation. As per the story, the Sky Vasu stole a cow that belongs to one noble sage called Vasishta. The sage got mad and cursed the Vasus to be born on earth as humans. They begged for forgiveness and the sage make the curse milder. He said that 7 of the Vasus will have short human life, but the Sky Vasu will need to have a full human experience. The 8 Vasus went to the river Ganges and asked her if she could be their mother. She agreed and became a beautiful woman. The son of the king fell in love with her and wanted to marry her – she agreed on one condition – the prince will never question her actions. He agreed. This woman got pregnant 7 times and each time she dropped her child in the water of Ganges to drown. When she carried her eighth child and prince shouted at her why she is doing it? The curse was fulfilled – 7 of the Vasus had short human life. She went to the prince, gave him the eighth child and she disappeared into the waters. Her eighth child was the Sky Vasu, who became Bhishma, important part of the Mahabharata.

So, Dhanishta nakshatra is not good for marriage and having children. It is associated with drowning and abortion.

Another deity related to Dhanishta is Shiva, who has immense musical talent. Shiva is famous for his dance, called tandava, and his Nataraja posture.

Key Points

1. Dhanishta natives will take the qualities of the eight Vasus – confidence, wisdom, victory, music talent, energy, radiance, joy, purity, and sensitivity. The Vasus may give them wealth, gems, gold, and prosperity.

2. Dhanishta natives may have issues with children or abortion. It is said that if these natives have abortions, they help a saint to pay

his karma like the river Goddess helped the 8 Vasus to clear their karma.

3. Dhanishta natives have karma with marriages - marriage may feel dry and without love or there can be delay or even deny of marriage. They have a karmic relationship with their siblings, too.

4. Dhanishta people are great warriors and ferocious fighters. They can have a demon inside of them. They can become great athletes in fighting sports, martial arts, like boxing for example.

5. Dhanishta natives are natural musicians! They love music, dancing, and sounds. They are visionary people with strong intuition.

6. Dhanishta people are very hardworking. They can be great doctors, police officers, sports figures, and if there is malefic influence - criminals. Dhanishta people can bully other people, or they can be bullied.

7. Dhanishta natives may have wealth and lands, and properties. They can be recognized in society and famous. However, they may need to go far away from their home to make this wealth.

8. Dhanishta natives should be careful with their promises – if they don't keep their promises, they will reincarnate back to Earth to fulfill that promise.

9. Dhanishta people will face a lot of fights, battles, and competitiveness. Early in life they may feel hollow inside and will try to fill the emptiness. They can be greedy, revengeful, and materialistic

10.   If there is malefic influence, Dhanishta male natives may hate women and act aggressively.

11.   These people have a youthful appearance

12.   According to my teachers, Dhanishta natives may get married between the age of 26 and 28.

13.   These people are good at timing – they know the rhythm of time.

14.   Dhanishta natives have qualities of a lioness – they are the "hunters of the pride ", which means they are the providers in the family. They will be the engine of the family. Their spouse will be a protector like the male lion, but the main figure will be the Dhanishta native.

15.   Dhanishta people will also have to fight a major war in their life, either in court, personal combat, or society.

16.   Dhanishta natives should not steal anything – they will be always captured and punished.

Remedies

The best remedy for this nakshatra is to sing or play a musical instrument, especially a drum or flute. Another remedy is to practice a martial art or buy a bass statue of a lioness.

This nakshatra is associated with the rhythm of time, so if you have a clock that it is not working, you have to fix it immediately.

If you have prominent Dhanishta in your chart maybe it will be better not to officially get married- you can still have family and everything and live in love and harmony, but you can skip the official signature. Of course, this depends on the whole horoscope – you can always contact me for a reading on my website : www.astrology-coaching.com . All my clients with Dhanishta complained about their marriage.

Careers/Hobbies

Dhanishta nakshatra may produce professions (or hobbies) related to:

- All professions related to music and dancing
- Entertainment industry
- Enforcement, military, and police
- Martial arts and athletes
- Medical fields and healing
- Real estate and lands,
- Jewelry
- Professions associated with wealth and money
- Managers of all kinds

Examples

I will give you an example with one of my clients, who booked a detailed horoscope reading with me.

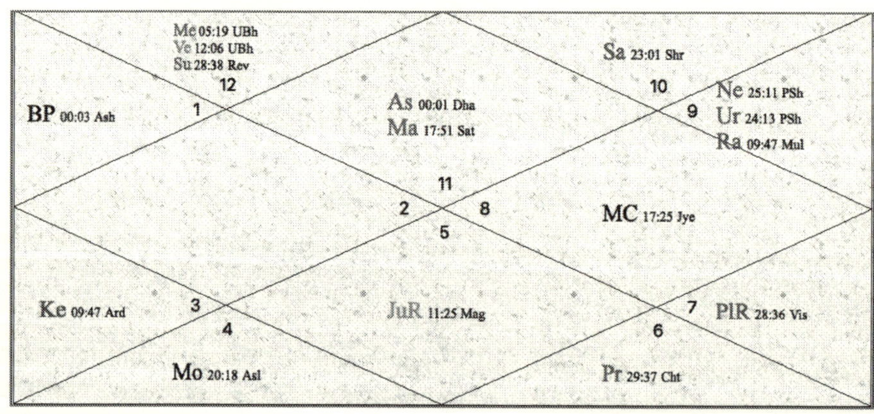

He has an Ascendant in Dhanishta. Although he is not professional, he loves music and dancing – he told me that he is constantly listening to music and singing old Arabic and Jewish songs. Maybe the kind of song comes from the influence of Rahu in Aquarius, which is connected with Muslim culture. The other thing is he loves wristwatches and had one broken, so I told him to fix it or throw it because it will bring him bad luck. The interesting thing was that he loved gems, jewels, and especially yellow diamonds. In the beginning, I thought the reason for that is the multiple conjunctions in the second house, but then I remembered that the stars of Dhanishta nakshatra are forming the Delphinus constellation, which has a diamond shape in the sky, and Dhanishta natives love gems and diamonds.

SHATABHISHA

The Hundred Stars

ZODIAC RANGE	6°40' AQUARIUS - 20°00' AQUARIUS
RULING PLANET	RAHU
DEITY	VARUNA
SYMBOL	EMPTY CIRCLE
CASTE	BUTCHER
ANIMAL	FEMALE HORSE
SOUNDS	GO, SAA, SEE, SOO
MAIN FIXED STARS	GAMMA AQUARI, PISCIS AUSTRINUS
PADAS	PADA 1- SAGITTARIUS PADA 2- CAPRICORN PADA 3- AQUARIUS PADA 4- PISCES
COLOR	BLUE GREEN
GENDER	FEMALE NAKSHATRA/NEUTRAL
KEY WORDS	SECRETS, SECLUSION, HEALING, PHILOSOPHICAL

Meaning

Shatabhisha (or Shatabhishak) is the twenty-fourth nakshatra in the zodiac belt. It lies entirely in the zodiac sign of Aquarius. So, here you can feel the energies of Aquarius, Saturn, and Rahu, which is not only the co-ruler of Aquarius but is the ruler of the nakshatra, too. This is one of the most Rahu-influenced nakshatras. Rahu is the demon's head, which wants all the material success and pleasures, it is our mission on this planet. There is a dark demonic energy in Shatabhishak nakshatra. Natives are part of 2 worlds – dark and bright. They should tame the demon inside of them and transform it. Definitely, Shatabhishak nakshatra is not an easy nakshatra. The combination of Saturn-Rahu will require a lot of work and discipline. The ego has to be broken and worldly attachments destroyed. Shatabhishak people will have to fight the negative forces within. Despite this dual world, Shatabhishak can produce one of the most unique, out-of-the-box, and eccentric people – futuristic beings, who are part of the New World and technologies. Shatabishak is the core of the Aquarius zodiac sign.

Shatabhishak translates into "hundred physicians", and "hundred healers". The alternative name is Shatataraka, which means "possessing a hundred stars". This tells us that Shatabhishak is dealing not only with healing and medicine but with the stars and universe. The symbol of this constellation is an empty circle. This can mean a magical charm or a symbol of infinity – there is no beginning and no end. The alternative symbol is a hundred stars, which again shows us a deep connection with the sky and the cosmos. It is associated with our past karma, too. Shatabhishak people should reach the highest understanding of their spiritual path. The animal is a female horse. The horse is strong, fast, and beautiful. It can be both free and tamed. The same is with Shatabhishak natives – they can be free and tamed, too. We associate the horse with Hayagriva, who is human with a horse head – the god of knowledge and wisdom.

Shatabhishak is a nakshatra of justice, fair treatment, and revolutionary forces in human society. It is related to underground groups and movements. It is related also to aerospace and the atmosphere.

This nakshatra is also associated with unveiling the secrets from the hidden realms and disclosing the knowledge of the occult.

Deity

The ruling deity of Shatabhisha is **Varuna**, the God of oceans and Cosmic Law. This constellation is related to oceans, seas, rivers, rain, and all types of liquids, even alcohol. Varuna is similar to the planet Neptune. Varuna, resembling the Aquarius sign, is depicted holding a pot, which contains Soma, the elixir of power and youth that Gods drink. Additionally, Varuna can be depicted with medicinal herbs, which are associated with healing on all levels – physical and astral. Varuna's herbs not only heal, they rejuvenate, too.

Varuna rules the night because the night is the cosmic ocean. It is said that Varuna has 1000 eyes and the stars in the sky are his eyes.

This deity rules both the law and the underworld, so he has 2 sides – bright and positive and dark. He is to the underworld what Indra is to the Heavens. Varuna is linked to the dark Sun, sunset, and West direction. Varuna is called the chief of demons, although he is not a demon, but God. He is a son of Aditi and part of the Adityas.

Varuna is also the God of Sin, Debts, Injury, and Disease, who not only brings these calamities upon people but can also remove them.

Key Points

1. Shatabhisha natives have a dual nature – they always have a bright and dark side. In order to be happy they need to destroy their demon inside. The Shatabhisha natives counter difficult karmas.

2. Shatabhishak natives are always attracted to astronomy, stars, the cosmos, secrecy and secret societies, aliens, UFOs, and conspiracy theories. This nakshatra may produce astronauts. They may face some unusual or paranormal events in their life, too, especially if Rahu, Ketu, Saturn, or Moon are placed in this constellation.

3. These people can be great doctors, physicians, and healers. Herbs, oils, and bud flowers can be very beneficial for them. They are healers of the physical and spiritual/ mental world. After the age of 42, they will be more interested in Ayurveda than traditional medicine.

4. Shatabhisha natives are interested in Persian, Greek, or Muslim culture. They may love South America

5. Due to the myth of Varuna and Mitra, who fell in love with the same woman, Shatabhisha natives will be involved in a love triangle. One of these persons may have strong Anuradha nakshatra

6. One of the children of Shatabhisha (or Anuradha) natives can be a very spiritual

individual – something like a guru/sage. This comes again from the myth of Mitra and Varuna. The woman they loved gave birth to two sages

7. Like all horse-associated nakshatras, Shatabhisha natives love their hair and pay attention to how they look externally. They may have strong bodies, especially legs. They may work in fields related to hair, external appearance, body, and fitness. They may love horses, too

8. They like to cut things and reconstruct them. They are impatient people and want things to be done fast. Unfortunately, they will need to learn to be patient, due to Saturn.

9. Shatabhisha natives love circles or drawing circles/ holes.

10. Shatabhisha natives may have a tattoo on the neck or the back

11. Shatabhishak natives are revolutionary people and can change society. They are out-of-the-box, independent, mysterious, secretive, and allure people. These natives fight for justice and different causes.

12. They can have a bad relationship with their father – Varuna cursed his father.

13. They can be very good at music and spirituality – this comes from the fixed star Piscis Austrinus (Fomalhaut)

14. Shatabhishak people have an interest in esoteric and occult subjects such as astrology, holistic sciences, tantra, alternative healing, modern research in technology, etc.

15. If there is a strong malefic influence in this nakshatra, there can be suicide thoughts or even committing suicide through hanging. This is due to the symbol of the constellation which is a circle. Often, if these natives got sick, they would need to go to "100 doctors" to find out what is going on with their health. It is recommended to find a doctor with a strong Ashwini nakshatra.

16. These people love (or afraid of) water and are interested in liquids. If there are malefic planets, the natives can become alcoholics/ drug addicted or there can be intoxication. They may love flowers and plants, too – some astrologers say that the alternative symbol is not 100 stars, but 100 flowers.

17. Shatabhishak natives are growing fast. They can be working in fields, associated with science, religion or philosophy, electricity and electronic communication, media, and technology.

18. Loneliness, apathy, self-pity, depression, isolation, and a feeling of being restrained or restricted may be experienced by the natives. They can hide their soul and emotions from others. They have boundaries and don't let other people easily in their circle.

19. There can be some theme with crocodiles because Varuna rides a crocodile.

Remedies

Some of the remedies for this constellation are to have a brass statue of a horse, ride a horse or live next to water. The other option is to study astrology or astronomy or have your own herbs and plants.

You can also have a small fountain in your house.

Careers/Hobbies

Shatabhishak nakshatra may produce professions (or hobbies) related to:

- Water and marine life

- Astrology, spirituality, and occult

- Medicine and healing

- Media and communication

- Electricity and electronics

- Aerospace, astronomy, and cosmos

- Philosophy

- Alcohol and liquids

- Technology and Research

- Professions associated with secrecy

- Professions associated with revolutions and strikes, organization of events.

- Science

Examples

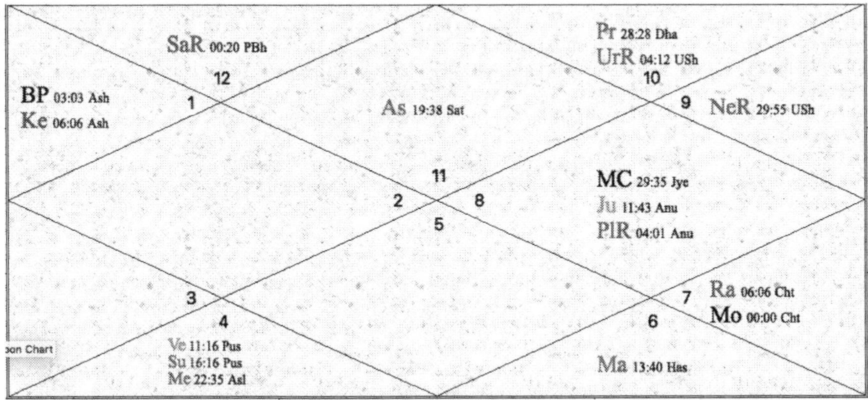

I will give you an example of one of my clients, who booked a consultation with me. She has an Ascendant in Shatabhishak nakshatra.

The first manifestation of Shatabhisha is that she loves horses and horse riding. The other thing is that she is interested in astronomy and astrology and always wanted to study the stars and the cosmos, which is typical for this nakshatra. She is into spirituality a lot, but as you can see, she has Jupiter in Scorpio, and Saturn in Pisces, so it's normal to be a more spiritually and occult-inclined person. She faced a lot of turmoil in her life and had to face the demon inside her to get to her spiritual path – she had depression and suicidal thoughts. Now she takes part in different big organizations for helping society, which is a typical Aquarius theme.

PURVA BHADRAPADA

The Burning Star

ZODIAC RANGE	20°00' AQUARIUS - 3°20' PISCES
RULING PLANET	JUPITER
DEITY	AJA EKAPADA
SYMBOL	SWORD
CASTE	BRAHMIN
ANIMAL	MALE LION
SOUNDS	SAY, SO, DA, DE
MAIN FIXED STARS	MARKAB, SCHEAT
PADAS	PADA 1- ARIES PADA 2- TAURUS PADA 3- GEMINI PADA 4- CANCER
COLOR	SILVER
GENDER	MALE NAKSHATRA
KEY WORDS	DARK SIDE, TRANSFORMATION, FIRE, PASSION

Meaning

Purva Bhadrapada is the twenty-fifth nakshatra in the zodiac belt. It overlaps two zodiac signs – Purva Bhadrapada starts at 20°00' Aquarius and ends at 3°20' Pisces. The first part of the constellation is influenced by Aquarius, Saturn and Rahu, together with Jupiter, which is the ruling planet of this nakshatra. The second part is influenced by the energies of Pisces and Jupiter, which is both ruler of the zodiac sign and the constellation.

What is Pisces? Pisces is the most spiritual zodiac sign – it rules not only spirituality but other dimensions, dreams, imagination, isolation and escape, fantasies, traveling, oceans and seas, healers, gurus, artists and writers, yoga, losses, forgiveness, and endings. It is a very sensitive, peaceful, and impractical sign. Jupiter is a guru and will bring knowledge, wisdom, and expansion to this constellation. In the Aquarius part, first you will see more responsibility and restrictions, before the expansion – you have to work for the growth. In the Pisces part, you will see higher spiritual inclination. Don't forget that all Jupiter-ruled nakshatras are heavy and give karmic lessons, so Purva Bhadrapada is not an exception to that rule. Purva Bhadrapada is a serious star with significant personal transformation.

Purva Bhadrapada means "the first blessed feet", "the former lucky feet" or "beautiful left foot". It is associated with blessings from the past life karma. The main symbol is a sword – it can be used for defense and attack! The sword is related to fighting for a cause, for a special reason and it can be used for different royal and religious ceremonies. Alternative symbols of this constellation are the "front part of a funeral cot" and "a man with 2 faces". The first symbol is related to death and the end of the human's earth existence. The second symbol shows us again the duality of this nakshatra – one of the faces is calm, and the other is mad and violent.

The animal of this constellation is a male lion. The lion is the king of the jungle. We associate this animal with strength, power, status, beauty, and protection. Purva Bhadrapada natives can be in positions of power and high status in society. The lion is connected to the Goddess Durga, who fights a war against a demon. So the theme of fighting and war is seen in this constellation, too.

Purva Bhadrapada consists of two main stars in the constellation Pegasus - Markab and Scheat. Markab is around 29° Aquarius and it is said to be a star of honors and success, however gives great sorrow, too. Scheat is around 5° Pisces and gives poetic abilities, with extreme misfortune.

Deity

The ruling deity of Purva Bhadrapada is **Aja Ekapada**, which translates to "the one-footed goat" or "the unborn one-footed" – Aja means unborn, Eka- one, Pada -feet. Aja Ekapada is a goat-headed creature with one leg. It is associated with the dark and evil side of the world. Aja Ekapada can be seen in modern Western civilization – for example, all secret societies like Illuminati consider the goat god as their ruling deity, you can see this creature on the tarot cards, too.

Aja Ekapada is associated with black magic, spells, bones, and skulls, all kind of dangerous places.

Aja Ekapada has an ugly and strange appearance, so Purva Bhadrapada people may feel ugly and strange due to this fact – image problems and lack of self-love can be seen here.

Some astrologers have different theories about the ruling deity of this constellation. They believe that Purva and Uttara Bhadrapadas are ruled by two Nagas – Purva is ruled by the fire naga Ajaikapat and Uttara is ruled by the water naga Ahirbudhnya. Ajaikapat is one of the Rudras and is considered to be the mount of Lord Agni, the God of Fire. This dragon is associated with the fire that is connected with funerals and can be considered to be the spiritual fire that purifies the soul. He is also connected with lightning, winds, storms, and extreme occult groups like the Aghoris.

The common trait of both theories is that Purva Bhadrapada has strong destructive powers and a fiery temperament. It is associated with death and reincarnation, dark worlds. Often, the natives don't feel happy in this world, and they cannot connect with the earthy way of living.

It is observed that most homicides, mass murders, and genocides have some association with this nakshatra. This is a transformation-based nakshatra where the natives may sacrifice themselves for a higher cause and make a difference in the world.

Shiva/Rudra is another deity associated with this nakshatra.

Key Points

1. Purva Bhadrapada is one of the most unpredictable and dangerous nakshatras

2. Purva Bhadrapada natives can get obsessed with things. If they have a goal- they will forget everything else, till they achieve that goal. They will do everything to succeed in this task - for example, if these natives want to learn how to make YouTube videos, they will leave everything aside and start reading all possible sources, contacting all possible people, etc., till they learn how to make great YouTube videos. This has a good and a bad side. Purva Bhadrapada should find the balance, otherwise, this

obsession can cause a lot of pain... They are not superficial people and always go into the deep.

3. Purva Bhadrapada natives are like 2 different people in one body – one is kind, the other is evil. One of the most important tasks in the life of Purva Bhadrapada people is to find the balance between these two energies. The symbol of a man with two faces indicates the duality of the natives and a soul looking in two directions - one looking backward at the former life and one looking forward towards the next.

4. Natives with Purva Bhadrapada nakshatra may either be twins or will have twins in their family. Or have twin personality- these people can often change their views, answers, personality, and mind.

5. Purva Bhadrapada people are interested in the occult and the dark evil world. They may experience things against their will and things like sleep paralysis, abduction from aliens, paranormal events, etc. They are attracted to items that are old and dead in the modern culture – like antiques for example. They have an interest in kundalini, magic, aliens, and UFOs.

6. Purva Bhadrapada people are interested in secret societies and in the forbidden or hidden knowledge. These people may feel exiled from society.

7. Purva Bhadrapada people may have body image problems and insecurities. There can be extremes in sexual field and phobias.

8. Similarly, to their ruling animal – the male lion – these natives will be the leader of the pride. They will take a leadership role in the

community and protect it. Purva Bhadrapada natives are extremely protective of their families and children. Very often their spouse will be the main person responsible for the income of the family. This is because the lioness is the one who hunts the prey mainly.

9. Purva Bhadrapada people are interested in politics and all kinds of activism

10. There can be major leg injury or, generally said – any type of injury, so they have to be careful. Natives may have panic attacks too. These people are always attracted to natural medicine, herbs, and acupuncture.

11. These natives love to go to past life regressions. There is a karma from previous lives that they need to pay! This is an intense nakshatra that requires effort and discipline.

12. Whenever the natives of this constellation lend money, they will lose it. When they borrow money, this will bring them problems.

13. Other interesting traits of Purva Bhadrapada natives are that they are linked to Tibet and Buddhism, they like "heavy" music and they run away from everything that is part of the mainstream.

14. They love sports where legs are used more than the hands and they may love dragons, unicorns, snake-like creatures or creatures that are result of mutation.

15. Natives may love good food and may eat a lot. They may love mushrooms.

16. Purva Bhadrapada natives are radical, non-conformist, independent, passionate, impulsive, opinionated, with good speaking ability, and

skilled in making money. They can be very wise, too

17. Purva Bhadrapada natives feel directionless until they do something creative, political, medical, or some kind of activism.

18. These people may have hair like a lion's mane.

19. The natives of Purva Bhadrapada will love having a statue with wings in their homes – like a statue of an angel.

20. These people love doing investigations or love watching shows related to murder investigations.

Remedies

Some of the remedies for this constellation are to have a male lion statue in your home and read about aliens, and UFOs, the paranormal world. You should always pay respect to your dead relatives and friends and go to their funerals. Meditation is really important for this constellation.

You should avoid black magic and making spells and curses on other people.

Careers/Hobbies

Purva Bhadrapada nakshatra may produce professions (or hobbies) related to:

- All professions associated with death and funerals

- Medicine and healing

- Politics and activism

- Occult and mysticism

- The dark side of every profession or activity

- Police, defense, military, investigation

- Professions associated with extreme and fast actions

- Professions associated with Sci-Fi field

Examples

I will give you an example with one of my clients, who booked a detailed horoscope reading with me.

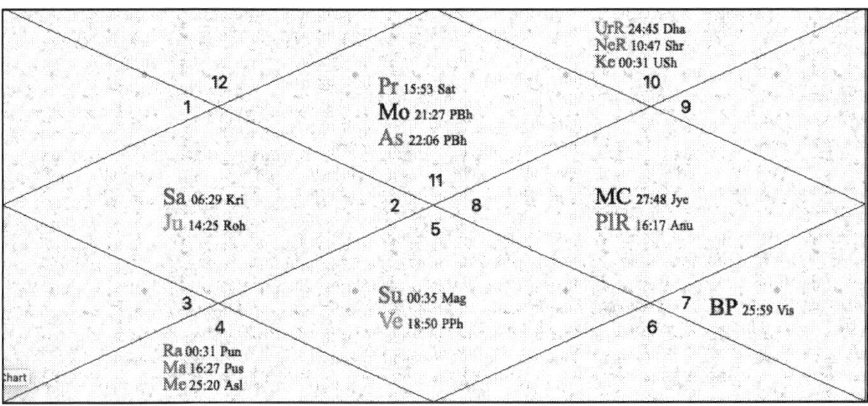

This individual has a Moon and Ascendant in Purva Bhadrapada, so definitely this nakshatra is very important for this horoscope. The client told me that she has never heard about nakshatras, and she was amazed at how accurately they described her life. The first manifestation was that she is crazy about UFOs and aliens and believed in black magic. She was always mesmerized by the secret society and dreamt to become part of the Illuminati. She is fascinated by the dark mystic side of the world. The other manifestation is that she had a past life regression, too, and always goes to fortunetellers to tell her the future.

UTTARA BHADRAPADA

The Warrior Star

ZODIAC RANGE	3°20' PISCES - 16°40' PISCES
RULING PLANET	SATURN
DEITY	AHIR BUDHYANA
SYMBOL	A SERPENT IN WATER
CASTE	WARRIOR
ANIMAL	FEMALE COW
SOUNDS	DU, THA, A, JNA
MAIN FIXED STARS	ALGENIB, ALPHERATZ
PADAS	PADA 1- LEO PADA 2- VIRGO PADA 3- LIBRA PADA 4- SCORPIO
COLOR	PURPLE
GENDER	MALE NAKSHATRA
KEY WORDS	ANGER, WATER, WISDOM

Meaning

Uttara Bhadrpada is the twenty-sixth nakshatra in the zodiac belt. It lies entirely in the zodiac sign Pisces. This constellation is influenced by the energies of Pisces, Jupiter, and Saturn, which is the ruler of that nakshatra. As you know, Saturn-ruled nakshatras are more beneficial for the natives. Saturn will give them blessings, however, first they will need to learn the lessons and follow the rules of Shani. The combination of Saturn and Jupiter in a spiritual sign like Pisces brings higher knowledge and spirituality. Jupiter will give wisdom to Uttara natives and Saturn will give material and spiritual rewards. Saturn will give the natives the ability to control their anger much better than Purva Bhadrapada.

Uttara Bhadrapada means "the latter blessed feet", or "the latter lucky feet". The name of the constellation is a result of the connection with the previous nakshatra - Purva Bhadrapada. Both Purva and Uttara Bhadrapada form a pair, which has similar traits. The main symbol of Uttara Bhadrapada is a serpent in deep water. This symbol is associated mainly with the deity of the constellation. Snakes are creatures with strong kundalini energy. Water is a symbol of life, coolness, and stillness. The alternative symbol is the back part of the funeral cot, which is again associated with death and exit from this world. There is another symbol – twins, which tells us that this nakshatra has a dual / twin personality, too. Purva and Uttara Bhadrapadas are associated with the myth of the two Bhadras – Bhadra Kali and Bhadra, the sister of Saturn. Purva is connected with Bhadra Kali – the auspicious form of Kali. Uttara is connected with the sister of Saturn -Bhadra, who is extremely aggressive and ferocious.

The animal of Uttara Bhadrapada is a female cow. Cows are the most sacred animals in India. They are related to fertility, prosperity, food, success, respect, and honor. Cows are associated with the five cows of Shiva

Deity

The ruling deity of Uttara Bhadrapada is **Ahir Budhanya**, another god associated with snake energy and Kundalini. Ahir Budhanya is the water naga, which sleeps at the bottom of the ocean. Ahi means serpent, and Budhan means bottom, so we can translate the name to "the snake from the bottom or depths". Most of the Vedic texts don't give a lot of information about this deity. We know that he is one of the 11 Rudras. Rudras are connected with the atmosphere. Ahir Budhanya is a more wise and compassionate deity in comparison to Aja-Ekapada. Ahir Bhudhanya is an auspicious naga that makes Uttara Bhadrapada manifest a love for water. Water is associated with life, fertility, spirituality and cleansing, and loneliness in some way. Ahir Budhyanya is the serpent who brings the rain, so Uttara Bhadrapada is associated with water and rains and hence, provides the necessary element for life support on Earth.

Lakshmi is another deity, associated with this constellation and provides prosperity and wealth. This nakshatra shows high intuitive energy in fields like poetry, music, dancing, writing, and counseling and inspires other people to follow them.

Key Points

1. Uttara Bhadrapada has similar traits to Purva Bhadrapada with one small difference – it is more calm and controlled. Uttara Bhadrapada natives are not as aggressive and fiery as the Purva Bhadrapada, and they simply want to deal with life in peace and quiet ambiance.

2. Uttara Bhadrapada is connected to the weather, and it is said that if these natives focus their energy, they will be able to control the weather.

People with prominent Uttara Bhadrapada very often can change the weather – if you have this nakshatra, pay attention if you think a lot of rain, whether it will start raining around you or not. Of course, you have to be connected with nature and use your kundalini energy. Uttara Bhadrapada relates to "vashyodyamana shakti"- the power to bring about the rain.

3. Uttara Bhadrapada natives have interests in aliens, UFOs, the occult, and death. They can have even paranormal experiences.

4. Uttara Bhadrapada people love desserts. They love oceans, ships, yachts, and stories about sea monsters and creatures. These natives love pearls, too.

5. They need to be in nature and surrounded by water and mountains to feel at peace.

6. These people can be prosperous. The natives may acquire wealth as a gift or inheritance, usually later in life.

7. Uttara Bhadrapada natives can be cheerful and generous, however, they can be aggressive and dangerous like Purva Bhadrapada natives

8. These people may have strong kundalini energy and psychic abilities and they should learn how to use them.

9. They are fascinated by the unknown world. They may have interests in the ocean bottom, mafia people and hidden secrets and societies, death and rebirth.

10. Uttara natives are extremely secretive about their wealth, connections, and skills. They may have hidden wealth. Nagas are treasury keepers, so these natives may be good at finance.

11.   Uttara Bhadrapada natives fight for causes like human rights, saving animals, etc. They can fight against human trafficking, criminality, and fraudsters, and fight against the underworld. They may have some connection to all crimes related to the underworld and grey financial sector like money laundering, money from fraud, gambling, drugs, darknet, etc.

12.   These natives can have twins or be a twin.

13.   Transformation plays a crucial role for the natives – like snakes they will need to change their skin and remove the old from their life.

14.   They can be extremely protective of their loved ones. They love solitude and seclusion, and they need time to contemplate. They may have neglected childhood and they may live far away from their place of birth

15.   They can be lazy and passive. There can be an event in their life that will change them forever.

16.   Uttara Bhadrapada people are deep personalities in every sense of the word – they have deep emotions, deep thoughts, deep depression, etc. This can lead to addictions and abuse

17.   Uttara Bhadrapada natives can be good counselors, astrologers, and occultists. They love writing and love fine art.

Remedies

Some of the remedies for this constellation are to have a fish aquarium in your house or a statue of a cow. You can live next to oceans or mountains where you can see everyday cows...something like the rural region of Switzerland.

If you feel nervous you can take a shower or listen to the sound of dolphins and other sea animals.

Careers/Hobbies

Uttara Bhadrapada nakshatra may produce professions (or hobbies) related to:

- Spirituality, meditation, and occult
- Professions related to the underworld
- Counseling and philosophy
- Art and spiritual communication
- Professions involving little movement
- Water and marine life
- Finance and wealth
- Nonprofit organization and charity

Examples

Some of the most famous representatives of this nakshatra are Barbara Streisand, Bruce Willis, and Elton John. All of them have an interest in the spiritual and occult world and have secretive life. They don't allow other people to intervene. They have incredible artistic talents and differ from the other singers/ actors. Bhadrapadas are always different from the masses and inside of them there is a fight of dual energies – good and evil, so that's why sometimes these people act as though they are a different person.

I want to share something with you – each nakshatra has its energy and I feel it even when I write the book. The most difficult nakshatras for writing were Jyeshta and both Bhadrapadas- honestly, they exhausted me entirely!

REVATI

The Wealthy Star

ZODIAC RANGE	16°40' PISCES - 30°00' PISCES
RULING PLANET	MERCURY
DEITY	PUSHAN
SYMBOL	FISH
CASTE	SHUDRA
ANIMAL	FEMALE ELEPHANT
SOUNDS	DE, DO, CHA, CHEE
MAIN FIXED STARS	ZETA PISCIUM, ETA PISCIUM
PADAS	PADA 1- SAGITTARIUS PADA 2- CAPRICORN PADA 3- AQUARIUS PADA 4- PISCES
COLOR	BROWN
GENDER	FEMALE NAKSHATRA
KEY WORDS	WEALTH, TRAVELING, NOURISHMENT, FERTILITY

Meaning

Revati is the last nakshatra in the zodiac belt – the twenty-seventh. It lies entirely in the zodiac sign of Pisces. Revati is influenced by the energies of Pisces, Jupiter, and Mercury, which is the ruler of this constellation. Mercury is the practical and analytical mind and here it goes deep into the impractical and dreamy Pisces. That's why Mercury is debilitated in this zodiac sign. If you have noticed Mercury rules all nakshatras that put an end to a cycle- Ashlesha, Jyeshta, and Revati- the mind forms a new reality! Pisces is a highly spiritual sign and Revati put the end of a period, but a new one begins – something is conceived in order to be born. Venus is exalted in Pisces.

Revati means "wealthy". This can be spiritual or material abundance. Revati people have a higher and deeper perspective, which leads to abundance. The issue with Revati natives is their high ideals and standards, which most people cannot match. This can make Revati people disappointed by the world around them because people cannot live up to their ideals. The symbol of Revati is a fish, swimming in water. It is directly related to the Pisces zodiac sign. We can associate this symbol with Vishnu, who transformed into the fish god, known as Matsya, to save the Vedas from the demon Hayagriva, who took them into the ocean. This tells us that Revati people are concerned about knowledge and the world around them. They are protectors and saviors of others. The fish is a high spiritual and religious symbol, which we can see not only in Hindu culture but in Christianity, too. Revati natives will find real happiness only if they are part of the ocean of spirituality. The alternative symbol of this constellation is a drum, the same symbol as Dhanishta. Both nakshatras are regarded as wealthy nakshatras. Revati's drum is associated more with the modern image of the drums, and it is associated with bringing information, and knowledge through music.

Music can be used for communication of your inner mental and spiritual world. I have prominent Revati nakshatra in my chart and when I make presentations or videos, I always involve music or there will be some kind of background music, which influence the audience.

The animal of Revati is a female elephant. The elephant is strong, powerful, fertile, productive, and very protective of their herd and babies. The elephant is a symbol of endurance, too. Revati's elephant is associated with the flying elephant, who interrupted the meditation of one sage and the sage cursed all elephants to walk on the ground. That is why Revati people sometimes don't feel happy living on the Earth, on this dimension – it is a curse for them to be locked on this planet, without having the wings to fly away to another world.

Revati professes to love, generosity, compassion, devotion, kindness, and non-violence. It is good nakshatra for marriage and love relationships.

Revati is associated with sunset and sunrise. Revati is one of the most beneficial nakshatras for spiritual growth and development of psychic abilities.

Deity

The ruling deity of Revati is **Pushan**, the nurturer. Pushan is a solar deity, one of the Adityas and he is the protector of flocks and herds, the deity of safe travels. Pushan is supposed to light up all paths and roads. He has a special affinity for animals – Pushan is the shepherd and veterinarian among Gods.

The name Pushan comes from the Sanskrit verb 'Pusyati', which means "one who causes people to thrive, one who brings bliss and prosperity"

Pushan guides both the living and the dead. He helps them to reach their final destination. He is the deity that sends the souls to the realm of Yama.

Pushan is the lord of lost things, so if you lose something, you may find it faster, when Moon transits in Revati. Revati people can bring back to their right places things or people that are lost. Pushan is the protector of travelers in their journey, he lights up the path, and he shows you the correct direction – these people know where others should go to find happiness and peace. If you feel without a path and direction, you should find a counselor with strong Revati nakshatra. I have noticed that all my clients who feel lost, are very happy and satisfied emotionally after consultation with me....because of the influence of my Revati - I "light up" their future roads like Pushan.

Revati natives should be careful with their teeth. As per the myth, Rudra knocked Pushan's teeth during the Daksha's sacred fire ceremony.

Pushan is depicted riding a goat-driven chariot. Goats are perfect climbers, so Revati natives know how to climb difficult terrains and walk dangerous roads in life– they are experts. Revati natives love exploring the world – meeting new nations and places.

Pushan is supposed to be a nourishing deity, that gives wealth and fruitful journeys.

<u>Princess Revati:</u>

The father of Princess Revati wanted to find the best spouse for his daughter, so they both went to search help from Brahma in the Brahma realm, but the god was sleeping. They waited for some time. When Brahma woke up, he asked why they were there. Her father said that he wanted to find a suitable bride for his daughter. Brahma said that here in this dimension time moves differently and while they were waiting, the centuries and yugas on the Earth changed, and their kingdoms have vanished. Modern people got shorter than what they were before. Brahma said that the only man suitable in this new era is Balaram, the elder brother of Krishna. Brahma made Revati shorter than her normal height, so she could match the new people on Earth.

This myth tells us that Revati natives have a theme associated with time and waiting. The other thing is that Revati natives will have either shorter spouses or much taller than them.

Key Points

1. Revati natives can be very successful and wealthy; however, they need to follow the spiritual path- this is the only road to happiness

2. Revati natives are kind, wise, clever, generous, loveable, compassionate people. They try to help all humans and animals – they are protectors of the herd in any sense! They are the divine shepherd!

3. These people are great counselors – they can light up the world of the lost souls

4. Revati people love animals – they can be part of organizations like PETA, and help foster animals, too.

5. Revati people love oceans and marine life and world – boats, ships, lighthouses, sea animals, cruises, etc. They love eating mashed food like mashed potatoes for example or they don't chew their food a lot.

6. Revati people love music, art, poetry, spiritual poetry, books of Rumi, etc.

7. Spirituality is an essential part of their life. They need to help people in need. They can be devotees of religion and Gods. They can be afraid of God.

8. Revati people love traveling. They have a theme associated with paths, roads, and life paths.

9. Revati natives can date extremely tall or shorter than them people. They may procrastinate on choosing their partner and miss out the perfect match

10. There may be a minor collusion between motor vehicles early in their life – a small catastrophe

11. Revati natives are known to be giving foster care to children or animals. Revati likes to guide and rescue those who deserve special protection. They are often seen in pediatrics, veterinary medicine, hospice work, emergency, animal activism, and protective shelters. They can adopt a child or an animal.

12. Revati people may live in a foreign country

13. If you do anything wrong to Revati or Bharani natives, the elephant-ruled nakshatras, they will remind you of what you did to them even after 20 years.

14. People with planets in this nakshatra may be confused in their early life about which path to take, and what decisions to make.

15. Pushan and Ashwin Kumaras are known for their ability to heal animals, so Revati natives are good veterinarians

16. Revati is the nakshatra of the dreamer, so these natives can create their own worlds. This

nakshatra doesn't have limits – it is connected with the transcendental. These natives always see the "big picture" and they have the ability to understand the other nakshatras. The natives of this constellation are like chameleons.

Remedies

Some of the remedies for this constellation are to live near water or travel to islands, go on cruises, and have a statue of an elephant with beautiful tusks and a trunk. You can play musical instruments or listen to music, too.

You should take care of your teeth because there is karma related to this theme.

Careers/Hobbies

Revati nakshatra may produce professions (or hobbies) related to:

- Water and marine life
- Spirituality and religion
- Travel and transportation industry
- Counseling
- Art and media
- Animals
- Professions associated with time

Examples

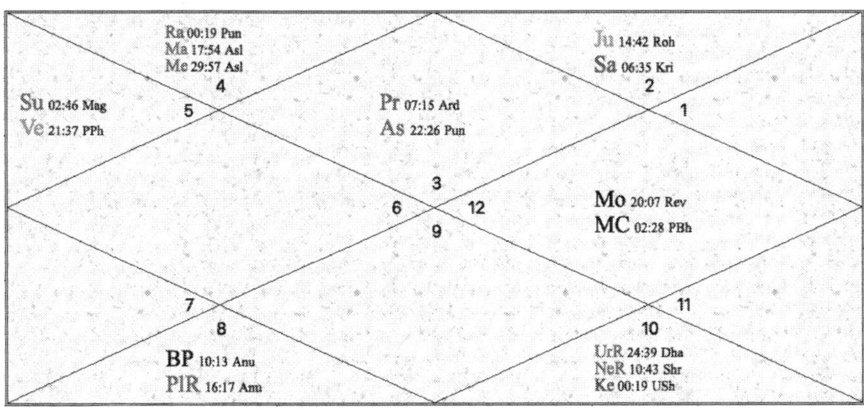

This is a chart of a client. She booked a career consultation with me. She has Moon in Revati. The first interesting manifestation of Revati is that this individual worked on a cruise ship for 1 year. The other interesting thing is that she loves oceans and swimming with dolphins and sea turtles. My client is interested in saving the planet and she is a supporter of PETA – People of Ethical Treatment of Animals. The other manifestation is that she used to date shorter men in her life, which is common for women with this nakshatra. She wants to have a YouTube channel about different spiritual topics and enlightenment of the people – all these are typical Revati manifestations.

THE FORGOTTEN NAKSHATRA

Abhijit

As I have mentioned at the beginning, there is another nakshatra system that uses not 27, but 28 constellations. I often call the 28th nakshatra – the forgotten nakshatra, but it is not forgotten at all...it is rather discarded than forgotten. Its name is Abhijit.

The twenty-eight constellation was discarded by Vedic gurus due to a few possible reasons. The first one is because the 27 nakshatra system fits better in the lunar calendar. The Moon makes one circle around the zodiac signs approximately for 27,32 days. The other possible reason is due to the length of the zodiac belt, which is 360°- it is impossible equally to divide the belt into 28 parts and each planet to rule 3 constellations.

Other Vedic scholars say that Abhijit is far north from the ecliptic and Moon never enters its area. Abhijit is the Sanskrit name for Vega, the brightest star in the northern constellation of Lyra.

There is a myth, associated with Abhijit, which says that sage Daksha had 27 daughters and one son. So, Abhijit is the brother of the 27 sisters and the only male nakshatra.

Abhijit lies approximately between 0° Capricorn - 11° Capricorn (in some sources it is around 6°- 11° /12° Capricorn) and takes parts from Uttara Ashadha and Shravana. Abhijit means "the undefeatable", or "conquering completely". It is very similar to Uttara Ashadha, which is also related to victory and triumph over enemies. So, if you have any planets in this degree span, they will give the same effect as Uttara Ashadha and Shravana.

Abhijit degrees are said to be one of the most powerful parts of the zodiac belt. According to the Vedic myths, Krishna removed this nakshatra from the belt, because it was so powerful and can be misused. However, Abhijit is not used in modern astrology. It is more of an added influence on the main 27 nakshatras than a separate constellation. I completely agree that this constellation is placed too north, and Moon cannot enter its area. If you have planets placed in the Abhijit degrees, you can have an extra powerful manifestation of their traits.

CHAPTER 5
UNEQUAL NAKSHATRA SYSTEM

In Vedic astrology, we use mainly the equal nakshatra system, which means that each nakshatra is 13°20'. However, there is an unequal nakshatra system with different lengths of the constellations. The system is not commonly used, still I wanted to share it with you, so you are aware. Please, at least at the beginning, it is recommended to use the equal system and later on, when you are an expert in the field of nakshatras, you can make your own research if this unequal system actually works.

- Ashwini is 13°20' long – from 0° to 13°20' Aries

- Bharani is 6°40' long – from 13°20' to 20° Aries

- Krittika is 13°20' long– from 20° Aries to 3°20' Taurus

- Rohini is 20°00' long – from 3°20' to 23°20' Taurus

- Mrigashira is 13°20' long – from 23°20' Taurus to 6°40' Gemini

- Ardra is 6°40' long – from 6°40' to 13°20' Gemini

- Punarvasu is 20°00' long- from 13°20' Gemini to 3°20' Cancer

- Pushya is 13°20' long- from 3°20' to 16°40' Cancer

- Ashlesha is 6°40' long– from 16°40' to 23°20' Cancer

- Magha is 13°20' long – from 23°20' Cancer to 6°40' Leo

- Purva Phalguni is 13°20' long – from 6°40' to 20° Leo

- Uttara Phalguni is 20°00' long – from 20° Leo to 10° Virgo

- Hasta is 13°20' long- from 10° to 23°20' Virgo

- Chitra is 13°20' long- from 23°20' Virgo to 6°40' Libra

- Swati is 6°40' long – from 6°40' to 13°20 Libra

- Vishakha is 20°00' long – from 13°20 Libra to 3°20' Scorpio

- Anuradha is 13°20' long – from 3°20' to 16°40' Scorpio

- Jyeshta is 6°40' long – from 16°40' to 23°20' Scorpio

- Mula is 13°20' long – from 23°20' Scorpio to 6°40' Sagittarius

- Purva Ashadha is 13°20' long – from 6°40' to 20° Sagittarius

- Uttara Ashadha is 20°00' long – from 20° Sagittarius to 10° Capricorn

- Shravana is 13°20' long- from 10° to 23°20' Capricorn

- Dhanishta is 13°20' long- from 23°20' Capricorn to 6°40' Aquarius

- Shatabishak is 6°40' long – from 6°40' to 13°20' Aquarius

- Purva Bhadrapada is 13°20' long- from 13°20' to 26°40' Aquarius

- Uttara Bhadrapada is 20°00' long – from 26°40' Aquarius to 16°40' Pisces

- Revati is 13°20' long – from 16°40' to 30° Pisces

CHAPTER 6
NAKSHATRAS MATCHMAKING

There are multiple techniques for checking the compatibility between two people and if they are a good match. In my online astrology course, called Online Astrology for Beginners, on the platform Thinkific, I have a special lesson for how to see events like having a child, promotion, synastry, and one about the nakshatras matchmaking, using the animal classification. I decided to share with you some insights in this book, too.

So now we are going to check the most compatible and most incompatible animal matches. Basically, in real life, you will see hundreds of animal combination options, where your effort will play an important role in preserving the relationship.

<u>Most Compatible:</u>

Of course, the most compatible is the pair of the same animal type – male lion with female lion, male buffalo with female buffalo, etc. This will be a perfect match of the energies of the couple. There always can be some issues – imagine if the girl is a male lion and the boy is a female lion...so here the energies will match, but the role in the relationship will be exchanged.

- Horse couple – Ashwini with Shatabhisha

- Elephant couple – Bharani and Revati

- Goat/sheep/ couple – Krittika and Pushya

- Snake couple – Rohini and Mrigashira

- Dog couple – Ardra and Mula

- Cat couple – Ashlesha and Punarvasu

- Rat couple – Magha and Purva Phalguni

- Cow couple – Uttara Phalguni and Uttara Bhadrapada

- Buffalo couple – Swati and Hasta

- Tiger couple – Chitra and Vishakha

- Deer couple – Jyeshta and Anuradha

- Monkey couple – Purva Ashadha and Shravana

- Lion couple – Purva Bhadrapada and Dhanishta

- Mongoose – there is no perfect match for Uttara Ashadha natives. They will need to learn how to create a relationship. Of course – we are speaking here for a perfect match. In real life – it is difficult to have perfect compatibility.

Most Incompatible:

Now I am going to share with you the animal pairs, which are not a good match and the relationship between these people will be difficult and they will need to work much more for keeping their love.

Strong incompatibility we see in:

- Cows with Tigers

- Cows with Lions

- Buffalos with Tigers

- Buffalos with Lions

- Snakes with Mongoose

- Cats with Rats

- Dogs with Deer

- Elephant with Lions

- Elephant with Tigers

- Horses with Buffalos

- Goats with Monkeys

Please keep in mind that we need to see the whole chart and use multiple other techniques to decide finally if this is a good match or not. When you are checking the animals of the nakshatras, you have to see the Ascendant, Moon, Venus, and Lord of the seventh house.

In real practice, most of the cases are a mix of other animal combinations. Yesterday, I had a couple, who came for synastry, and they had mongoose with goat, which is in the middle – it's not the most compatible, nor most incompatible combination. They already knew what the issues in their relationship are and they worked on fixing them because they loved each other.

Love is like a flower, you know, you have to water and nourish it to blossom and we, astrologers, we are like gardeners or the people who sell flowers in the shops – we can give you a few hints on how to take care of the flower.

CHAPTER 7
NAKSHATRAS MOTIVATION TECHNIQUE

Nakshatra Motivation Technique is related to the Dharma, Artha, Kama, and Moksha motivation of the constellations. I learned this technique from one of the most popular YouTube astrologers – Mr. Kapiel Raaj. I would say that this technique matches my personal life, so I hope it works for you, too.

Let's start! As you know, Dharma shows what is your mission or life purpose. Artha shows how you are going to earn your money. Kama shows how you will fulfill your desires and Moksha shows how you are going to find spiritual enlightenment.

To see your nakshatra motivation, you have to check the degrees of your Ascendant (First house). This degree point is the most important degree in each house in your horoscope.

- Your Dharma will be determined by the nakshatra ruler of your Ascendant.

- For your Artha, you take again the degrees of your Ascendant, but in the second house of your chart and see which is the nakshatra there. Its ruler will determine your Artha

- For your Kama, you take the degrees of your Ascendant again , but this time in the third house of your chart and see which is the nakshatra there

- For Moksha, you take the degrees of your Ascendant, but in the fourth house of your chart, and see which is the nakshatra and its ruler.

The first time, I heard this technique I asked myself why we take only the first four houses. The answer is simple – these are the first Dharma, Artha, Kama, and Moksha houses and the nakshatras lords will be repeating in the other houses – so, all Dharma, Artha, Kama, Moksha houses will have the same nakshatra lords.

If you are a 12° Gemini Ascendant, this means that your nakshatra is Ardra – so Dharma lord is Rahu. So, you have to check where in your chart is Rahu and analyze everything – what is Rahu, which house is placed, which sign and nakshatra, who is the ruler of the sign and the nakshatra, aspects, conjunctions, etc., and all this will give you information what is your mission in this life! If you see the other Dharma houses – 5th and 9th, you will realize that the 12° mark is again ruled by Rahu nakshatra, and the lord is repeating. The fifth house will be Libra – 12 degrees Libra is Swati, ruled by Rahu. The ninth house will be ruled by Aquarius – 12 degrees is Shatabhishak, ruled by Rahu again.

Example:

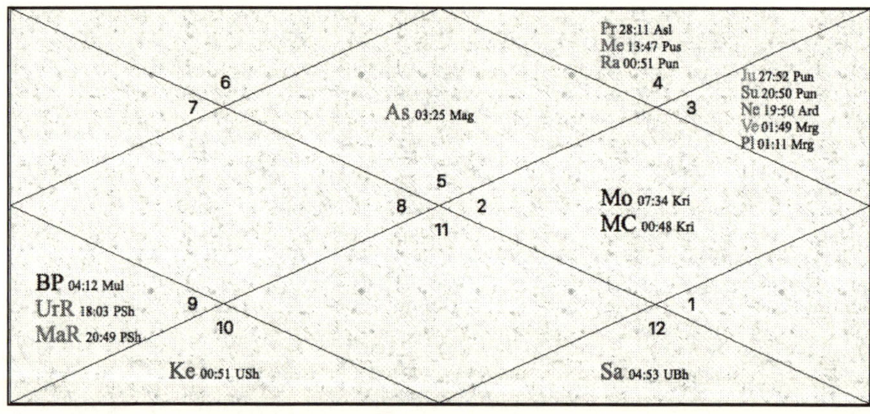

The degree of the Ascendant is 3°25' Magha nakshatra, Leo Zodiac sign.

- Dharma Lord will be the ruler of Magha – Ketu

- Now we are going to the second house and check the 3°25' point. Second house is ruled by Virgo and at 3°25' Virgo is placed Uttara Phalguni. Sun is the Artha Lord of this person

- We see the third house and 3°25' point. Third house is ruled by Libra and at 3°25' Libra is placed Chitra nakshatra. Kama Lord is Mars, which is the ruler of Chitra.

- We go to the fourth house - 3°25' Scorpio...we have to be careful here – it is Anuradha, which starts at 3°20' Scorpio. Saturn is the Moksha Lord.

Now you have to make a detailed analysis of each lord, so you can see the life purpose, income, fulfillment of desires, and spiritual evolvement of this person. I will mention a few words for each lord of the example above:

So Dharma lord is Ketu. Ketu will show us what will be the mission and the life path of this individual. Ketu is placed in the 6th house, Capricorn, Uttara Ashadha. Definitely, part of the life purpose of this individual is to face conflicts, problems, issues with health, enemies, debts, and even divorce. Ketu is detachment from the material world and catastrophic events. Uttara Ashadha is a later victory, so no matter what happens, this person will win the final battle.

Artha lord is Sun. Sun is placed in the 11th house, Gemini, Punarvasu. It is conjunct with Jupiter, Venus, Neptune, and Pluto, aspected by Mars. The Eleventh house is about fame, money, professional circles, famous and influential people, and big organizations. Gemini is about communication, media, art, skills of hands, and handmade art and craft. So, this person will earn money through all of this signification. This person may lose some money from the spouse – Venus is enemy of Sun, and it is conjunct with it. You have to take into consideration everything! Furthermore, it is good to check the positions of the Lords in Navamsa and Dasamsa charts.

Kama lord is Mars, and it is placed in the 5th house, Sagittarius, Purva Ashadha. Conjunct by Uranus, aspected by Sun, Venus, and Jupiter. The fifth house is the house of children, love and romance, and creativity. Purva Ashadha is connected with battle and wars, Mars is with Uranus, aspected by other planets, so definitely this individual will face problems fulfilling the desires. But love, creativity and children will pay crucial role.

Moksha lord is Saturn- 8th house, Pisces, Uttara Bhadrapada. Eight house is death, rebirth, accidents, sudden events, diseases, psychology, occult, and hidden world. Pisces is other dimensions, dreams, spirituality, loss. Uttara Bhadrapada is a dark constellation – the serpent from the ocean bottom. These elements will bring spiritual growth. However, this person definitely will face pain in life.

This was just a very short analysis, so I can show you the correct approach – you really need to go much deeper in the meaning of the houses, planets, signs, nakshatras, aspects, even padas. Now you can check your chart and your nakshatras motivations. Of course, you can always contact me for horoscope reading and I can make the full Motivation technique for you.

Just for your information, the example above is the chart of Frida Kahlo. You can read more about her in the open source and come back to the book and see if the motivation technique matches her life.

CHAPTER 8
NEXT STEP

Finally, we have reached the last chapter of the book, called Next step! First, I want to thank you for reading my book- I hope you learned a lot about my favourite topic in astrology – the nakshatras. I have put a lot of effort and love in the creation of "Nakshatras in Vedic Astrology-Easy&Simple" and I appreciate that you are part of my journey. Thank you!

Maybe this is the most appropriate time to thank all my clients, who had horoscope readings with me, because through their lives and personal experience, I gained more knowledge about astrology, nakshatras and their manifestations in the real life and I was able to write this book. Of course, I have to pay respect to all my Vedic teachers and the authors of the books I read, because they build my astrology background.

So, what is the next step for you? Firstly, you have to proceed to develop into the field of Vedic Astrology – you can go to astrology courses, read books, if you want to develop in the field of nakshatras it is essential to read the mythology of the Gods of the nakshatras. What is most valuable- you should definitely start making nakshatra readings to your friends and family and see how they manifest in their life.

If you want to have more professional approach, you need to start observing the transit of the Moon in the different nakshatras in your daily life. You have to see what kind of events happen, what kind of emotions you have or what kind of people you meet -everything matters. That's why I created the **"Nakshatras journal"**, which will help you writing down in an organized way the observation from each nakshatra.

Now, I want to share with you the resources I used for writing this book (apart from my astrological notes from clients and enrolled courses). You can start reading these books if you want to know more about the nakshatras:

1. *The Book of Nakshatras- A comprehensive treatise on the 27 constellations , by Prash Trivedi*

2. *The Nakshatras- The Lunar mansions of Vedic Astrology, by Dennis harness*

3. *The Nakshatras- The stars beyond the zodiac, by Komilla Sutton*

4. *27 stars, 27 Gods – the astrological mythology of Ancient India, by Vic DiCara*

5. *Research on nakshatras by Dr Arjun Pai*

6. *Nakshatras@Speed of light, by Kapiel Raaj*

About the Author

Anatoly Malakov is a certified Vedic astrologer, author, YouTuber, and spiritual coach. He combines the magic of Vedic Astrology with practical spiritual coaching and manifests his own "Astrology Coaching" spiritual practice. He believes that astrology is like a map that shows us the path and the future, however, we people still have free will. Through astrological coaching, we can take the most from our lives and fulfil our dreams.

Anatoly Malakov is the author of the "Easy & Simple" series for beginners in Vedic astrology:

- "Vedic Astrology- Easy&Simple" (book)

- "Vedic Astrology- Easy&Simple- The Notebook"

- Astrology Notebook

- "Nakshatras in Vedic Astrology – Easy&Simple"

- "Nakshatras Journal"

He is the author of spiritual coaching journals like:

- Coloring Gratitude Journal: The Power of Gratitude Combined with Color Therapy and Positive Affirmations

- Diario de gratitud y Colorear (Spanish edition)

- Dating Journal: Rate and Assess Your Love Dates

He is the creator of a special simplified Vedic astrology course for beginners with pre-recorded videos, which is the online continuation of the "Easy&Simple" approach.

Online Video Course for beginners in Vedic Astrology - https://astrologycoaching.thinkific.com/

For contact and horoscope readings, please refer to:

- website - https://astrology-coaching.com/

- email: astrology.coaching1@gmail.com

- YouTube channel - Astrology Coaching by Anatoly

- Facebook - Astrology Coaching by Anatoly